Welcome

In 1967, at the age of seven, I took a cycle ride with my father from our home at Three Bridges to East Grinstead. A scorching summer's day, we bought a drink and sought refuge in the cool shade of East Grinstead station booking hall. Walking through to the platforms the memory remains with me. Here were the trappings of a 'real' station of the type that had already been lost through 'modernisation' on the Brighton line stations that I was used to. For here was an abundance of green enamel signs, gas lighting, 'Brighton' platform benches, target signs, real clocks and a real signal box and green 'thumpers'.

Joining the Bluebell Railway seven years later, a project had just been announced regarding the intention of the railway to extend its line to East Grinstead. Little would I have known then that come the completion of the project 38 years later I would be editing the society's house magazine *Bluebell News* – or that East Grinstead would be on its second replacement station since 1967. A little bit of that earlier memory returned when, in Bluebell's 50th anniversary year in 2010, we left East Grinstead at night – in a green (Hastings) 'thumper' – pulling away from a platform with the same style lamp posts, target signs and real benches – and it wasn't a dream!

Culled from the pages of *Bluebell News* over the years, we present here the salient parts of the long story that is the northern extension project – as well as some material from the Bluebell Archive that would have been deemed 'sensitive' at the time and not hitherto published. May I thank the many members who have contributed material for this volume, in particular early member Chris Cooper for access to his photos and press cuttings collection; Mike Grant, a former member of the Extension Committee and Mike Esau, who was Bluebell's 'official photographer' up to the Kingscote stage of the extension project. But the biggest thanks has to go to the 10,600 members of the Bluebell Railway Preservation Society and its volunteers and management, Bluebell plc shareholders, staff and contractors and the generous members of the visiting public – all of whom have given time, funds and labour to see this project through.

Colin Tyson
Editor

'The Improbable Restoration'

C000071962

Colin Tyson

The 43-year battle to extend the famous Bluebell Railway to East Grinstead

A BLUEBELL NEWS SPECIAL PUBLICATION

Editor:
Colin Tyson

Designer:
Rosie Ward

Reprographics:
Jonathan Schofield
Simon Duncan

Group production editor:
Tim Hartley

Production manager:
Craig Lamb

Marketing manager:
Charlotte Park

Publisher:
Dan Savage

Commercial director:
Nigel Hole

Managing director:
Brian Hill

Published by:
Mortons Media Group Ltd,
Media Centre,
Morton Way, Horncastle,
Lincolnshire LN9 6JR
Tel: 01507 529529

Printed by:
William Gibbons and Sons,
Wolverhampton

ISBN 978-1-909128-26-2

Glossary of Abbreviations used

AGM	Annual General Meeting
BR	British Railways/British Rail
BRPS	Bluebell Railway Preservation Society
CPO	Compulsory Purchase Order
DEMU	Diesel Electric Multiple Unit
DOE	Department of the Environment
DOT	Department of Transport
ED	Electro-Diesel
EGTC	East Grinstead Town Council
FOK	Friends of Kingscote
GBRf	Great Britain Railfreight
LBSCR	London, Brighton & South Coast Railway
LEGR	Lewes and East Grinstead Railway
LRO	Light Railway Order
LSWR	London & South Western Railway
MSDC	Mid Sussex District Council
NFU	National Farmers Union
S&C	Switches and Crossings
SER	South Eastern Railway
WSCC	West Sussex County Council

MORTONS
MEDIA GROUP LTD

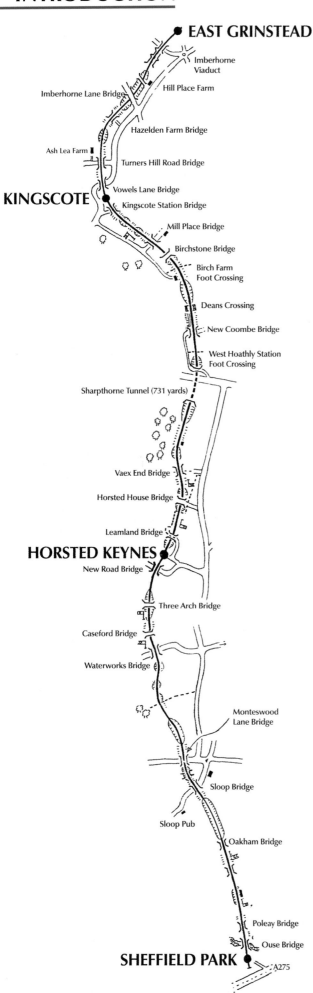

EAST GRINSTEAD
Imberhorne Viaduct
Hill Place Farm
Imberhorne Lane Bridge
Hazelden Farm Bridge
Ash Lea Farm
Turners Hill Road Bridge
Vowels Lane Bridge
KINGSCOTE
Kingscote Station Bridge
Mill Place Bridge
Birchstone Bridge
Birch Farm Foot Crossing
Deans Crossing
New Coombe Bridge
West Hoathly Station Foot Crossing
Sharpthorne Tunnel (731 yards)
Vaex End Bridge
Horsted House Bridge
Leamland Bridge
HORSTED KEYNES
New Road Bridge
Three Arch Bridge
Caseford Bridge
Waterworks Bridge
Monteswood Lane Bridge
Sloop Bridge
Sloop Pub
Oakham Bridge
Poleay Bridge
Ouse Bridge
SHEFFIELD PARK
A275

The Nortl

by Mike Grant/Colin Tyson

RE-OPENED by volunteers in 1960, after 12 years of running steam trains on the Bluebell Railway with ever-increasing success, purchasing the five-mile line from Sheffield Park to Horsted Keynes from British Railways and laying down improved facilities for its locomotive and carriages, it was only natural that thoughts should turn to expansion of the line in its second decade.

Following expired planning permissions made in the latter part of 1972 to extend to Horsted House Farm, it was in 1975 that the former station site at West Hoathly on the route of the closed railway line between Horsted Keynes and East Grinstead came up for sale. It immediately stirred Bluebell's interest – for if the site succumbed to housing development it would block the route north forever. With an extended mortgage, Bluebell Railway Ltd managed to purchase the site and from that day forth thoughts were channelled to see if it was possible to rebuild the whole line to East Grinstead. There was some local interest so surveyors for the Bluebell Railway were asked to prepare plans and submit an application to rebuild the line

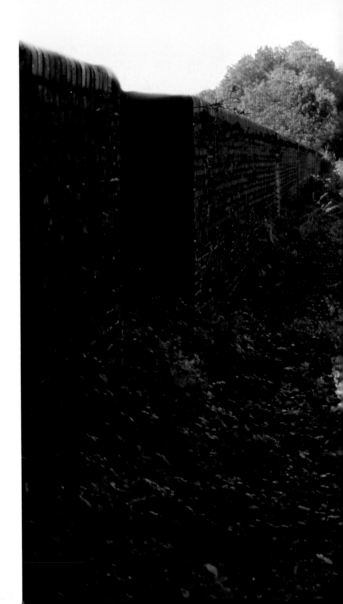

completely, from the north end of Bluebell's property at Horsted Keynes to join with British Rail at East Grinstead with a station of their own in the goods yard adjacent to the BR station. It was submitted to Mid Sussex District Council in 1978, then referred to a joint committee (of district and county planners) and rejected by three votes to two.

That lost vote was to cost Bluebell dear in time and money, forcing a Public Inquiry against the refusal and applying for a Light Railway Order at the same time. It was going to be the beginning of one the largest rebuilding projects ever carried out by a volunteer-run heritage railway. A leap of faith into the dark which was to take many years to realise.

Fortunately the Grade II Listed viaduct at East Grinstead had survived but the rest of the line had been taken apart and disposed of. Kingscote station survived but West Hoathly had not. Imberhorne Cutting, the largest and deepest on the line and cut from Wealden Ironstone was filled with East Grinstead's refuse and covered over with clay capping and sandstone from the excavations to construct the Beeching Way bypass to East Grinstead town centre.

After the line closed it had been divided up and sold off in lots, some 30 in all, to local land owners and farmers who used the trackbed as farm tracks or access ways. At Horsted House Farm the owner allowed the local rifle club to build a wall under the bridge as a butt and backstop for their rifle range. Some footpaths were diverted on to the trackbed and barbed wire fence barriers were erected to prevent trespassing. In a cutting north of Sharpthorne trees fell and created a dam – and the cutting had become flooded and impassable. Otherwise the formation had not suffered as much as some other lines had, as embankments could not be removed to join two fields together, so when it came to reconsidering rebuilding the line the only real obstacles, apart from the very real one of purchasing plots of land, was rebuilding one bridge at West Hoathly and removing the mountain of capped domestic waste that had completely filled Imberhorne Cutting.

Bluebell considered this a chance that must be taken, in order to regain a main line connection once again with the national network. Every effort had to be made to push forward to East Grinstead.

Abandoned from being used as a carriage stock siding by British Rail, following electrification of the line to East Grinstead, the deck of Imberhorne Viaduct slumbers in October 1993. MIKE ESAU

Pioneering and Consolidation

Opening Day crowds on 7 August 1960. Note the BBC TV cameraman on the canopy roof! BLUEBELL ARCHIVE

In order to put the Bluebell Railway's six-mile northern extension project in context, it is necessary to make a brief return to the whole Bluebell project in its historic sense. The Lewes and East Grinstead Railway Act, 1877, which was promoted by the Earl of Sheffield and other local landowners, authorised the construction of a railway between the towns mentioned, and the 1878 Act provided for the acquisition,

The four student founders of the Bluebell Railway were reunited on 17 June 2009. Railway chairman Roy Watts (centre) is seen with (from left) David Dallimore (now living in Toronto), Alan Sturt, Chris Campbell and Martin Eastland. COLIN TYSON

completion and running of the new line by the London, Brighton and South Coast Railway Co.

Opened in 1882, the line led a pretty unremarkable life as a rural secondary route between two market towns and the movement of produce over people took timetabled preference. Except for Barcombe, none of the intermediate stations were situated close to the villages they served and the busiest the line would have been

is when the Earl of Sheffield was hosting a cricket match at Sheffield Park, often attended by royalty.

With the progression of the internal combustion engine after the Second World War and the rise in usage of motor buses that served the villages better and lorries for door to door cartage, British Railways first proposed to close the route from Lewes to East Grinstead in 1954. This provoked outrage from the local residents – the very residents that had abandoned their 'beloved' line in droves in preference for private motor cars and other public transport.

Closure was approved early in 1955, to be effective from 28 May that year – in the event a railwayman's strike hastened closure.

Shortly after closure, eminent Chailey resident Miss Madge Bessemer discovered a loophole in the original Act pertaining to the line of 1877-78 relating to the 'statutory line' which forced a begrudging British Railways to reopen the route on 7 August 1956. It became known as the 'sulky service' – with single carriage trains calling at inconvenient times to just the four intermediate stations mentioned in the original Act – with Kingscote and Barcombe missing out. The British Transport Commission finally persuaded parliament to repeal the Act, thereby allowing British Railways to finally close the line on 17 March 1958.

Because of the unique nature of the 'double closure' there was much national TV and

The scene at Sheffield Park in 1960, prior to the public opening in August. The line's sole two coaches stand at the coal dock. Carriage painting was undertaken here, in the open air, until conditions improved some 12 years later with the erection of a 14-coach carriage shed at Horsted Keynes. BLUEBELL ARCHIVE

MINISTRY OF
TRANSPORT AND CIVIL AVIATION

HRC 914

Proposed withdrawal
of train services from the

Lewes—East Grinstead Branch Railway

Report of the Central Transport Consultative
Committee.

*Presented to Parliament by the Minister of Transport and Civil Aviation
by Command of Her Majesty
February 1958*

LONDON
HER MAJESTY'S STATIONERY OFFICE
TWO SHILLINGS NET

Cmnd. 360

newspaper attention afforded to what the press had dubbed the 'Bluebell Line' – and the time given to enact the second closure was enough space to let four students from Hove stage an inaugural meeting to gauge response to saving the 'Bluebell Line' and forming a preservation society.

David Dallimore, Alan Sturt, Martin Eastland and Chris Campbell held a meeting on 15 March, 1959, at the Church Lads' Brigade hall in Haywards Heath. Being 'juveniles' they asked local railwayman Bernard Holden, who had been born on the Bluebell Line in the stationmaster's house at Barcombe and was a leading light of the Burgess Hill Model Railway Club, to chair the meeting. It was Bernard Holden who, upon retirement from British Railways, came to the Bluebell full time, ultimately becoming its president until his death in 2012 aged 104.

On that day, the Lewes & East Grinstead Railway Preservation Society was founded and members were signed up. On 14 June, the society was formally constituted and a fundraising 'Bluebell Special' was held on 12 July, a railtour with a full complement of 280 seats from Tonbridge ran to East Grinstead and down the 'Bluebell' and back via Ardingly.

It soon became clear that it would be impracticable to save the whole line and so a middle section was chosen – there being water for engines at Sheffield Park – to a point just south of Horsted Keynes station (still worked by BR as the end of an electrified branch from Haywards Heath), and the booking office at Sheffield Park was rented from BR.

One has to remember that the Bluebell pioneers were the first to take on a redundant piece of former British Railways line with the aim of running steam trains on it and the Bluebell Railway Preservation Society (as it soon became called) had its motto of 'Floreat Vapor' – let steam flourish. The Talyllyn Railway in Wales had reopened with volunteers 10 years earlier and there was talk of the Ffestiniog Railway doing the same but no one had tried it with full size standard gauge equipment.

Much had to be done to be ready to open to the public on Sunday, 7 August, 1960, which was a great success, and society membership

Report of the Central Transport Consultative Committee regarding the proposed withdrawal of train services from the 'Lewes-East Grinstead Branch Railway', dated February 1958 and published just a month before the second closure.

now exceeded 1500.

With its small allocation of ex-LBSCR 'Terrier' and SECR P Class locomotives and meagre coaching stock – until the four ex-Metropolitan Railway coaches arrived from London Transport at a cost of £260 (the set) – the railway achieved a milestone when BR allowed it to run right into Horsted Keynes station from 29 October 1961,

Above: The first train at Bluebell Halt (Horsted Keynes) on opening day 7 August 1960, where a walk was then necessary by road for a few hundred yards to connect to Haywards Heath electric trains. BLUEBELL ARCHIVE

Left: Captain and Mrs Kimmins christen P Class No 323 *Bluebell* on opening day. BLUEBELL ARCHIVE

The makeshift halt at Horsted Keynes, complete with a drinks stall. From October 1961 British Railways allowed Bluebell to access Horsted Keynes station for cross-platform interchange. MIKE MORANT COLLECTION

Devoid of passenger shelter since Southern Railway cutbacks, the electric train waits to leave the 'electrified' platform at Horsted Keynes with a train for Haywards Heath and Seaford. BLUEBELL ARCHIVE

'Change here for the Bluebell Line'. Passengers alight from the electric train during the last season of the branch from Haywards Heath, 1963. BLUEBELL ARCHIVE

opposite the platform used by the electric trains to Haywards Heath and onwards to Seaford.

1962 saw the arrival of GWR 4-4-0 'Dukedog' No 9017 *Earl of Berkeley* in what was to become Bluebell's first and only GWR 'interloper' – privately preserved by Tom Gomm who had nowhere at that time to base the locomotive. North London Railway tank loco No 2650 then arrived, having ended its service on the Cromford & High Peak lines. LBSCR E4 No 473 *Birch Grove* also arrived and was to become a firm Bluebell favourite – another 'victory' for the 'Brighton' afficianados.

Several Maunsell coaches were purchased in 1963 to boost coaching stock but 1964 was a desperate year for Bluebell. The attitude from British Railways was fast hardening – basically Bluebell had to find the funds to purchase the line or be closed down. No money was available for anything else.

History can tell the story of the protracted negotiations with a hostile BR management and the final triumph came in 1968 when a hire purchase deal was struck, but there was a long and agonising period when it seemed that Bluebell's days were coming to a sad end.

One, and probably the only, highlight of 1964 was when, after the personal intervention of that famous East Grinstead resident, Dr Richard Beeching, LBSCR 'Terrier' No 32636 *Fenchurch* arrived. BR had given Bluebell just four weeks to acquire it but the 'Doctor' instructed that the loco should be reserved for six months. *Fenchurch* was to be the last of the Bluebell's locomotives to arrive 'in steam' via the Ardingly branch before the Bluebell was cut off from the national railway network – until 2010.

Thus the first five years of the Bluebell's operations came to a close under a dark cloud but, as we all know today, the struggle was not in vain and now the railway has possibly the finest collection of rolling stock to be seen on any heritage railway.

Much of the stock is not Bluebell-owned, but is there because the owners appreciate the facilities available. The work that has been done and the facilities and skills available at Horsted Keynes in being able to back-convert garden sheds, holiday bungalows and chicken coops to the glorious pre-grouping four- and six-wheeled passenger coaches that they once were is nothing short of miraculous.

'MARVELLOUS TO THINK IT IS SAFE FOR THE FUTURE'

Bluebell Railway is bought for £43,500

The line purchase of the Bluebell Railway was publicly confirmed at a short ceremony at Sheffield Park on 27 October 1968, when Frank Harrison, divisional manager of the Central Division of Southern Region, presented Bluebell general manager Horace May with a commemorative parchment marking the purchase of the Bluebell Line from British Rail for £43,500 – 'to include the station houses and 10 cottages at Sheffield Park and Horsted Keynes'.

With the line purchase completed, the railway was safe and it was time to concentrate on improving accommodation and facilities for restoring locomotives (at Sheffield Park) and carriages and wagons (at Horsted

Keynes); and plans for a locomotive works and a carriage works were soon under way.

By the end of the first decade, standard gauge railway preservation had started at the Keighley & Worth Valley Railway and the Severn Valley Railway – Bluebell was not alone any more but the line was paid for.

The original four students could not have envisaged the 32 locos, 60 carriages, 50 wagons, 50 full-time employees and 300 volunteers from a 10,600-strong membership that stands today. The pioneers of standard gauge preservation proved that they could 'Preserve the Puffer for Posterity'.

Above left: The framework for the new locomotive works under construction at Sheffield Park.
CHRIS COOPER

Above: It's hard to believe that this corner of the locomotive works is now a busy area – adjacent to the tramway for the loading of rolling stock by road. Another floor has recently been added to this elevation, to provide messing facilities for enginemen.
CHRIS COOPER

The last incoming railtour to take advantage of the connection via Ardingly and Horsted Keynes was the 'Blue Belle' railtour of 15 September 1963, seen here descending Freshfield Bank. MIKE ESAU

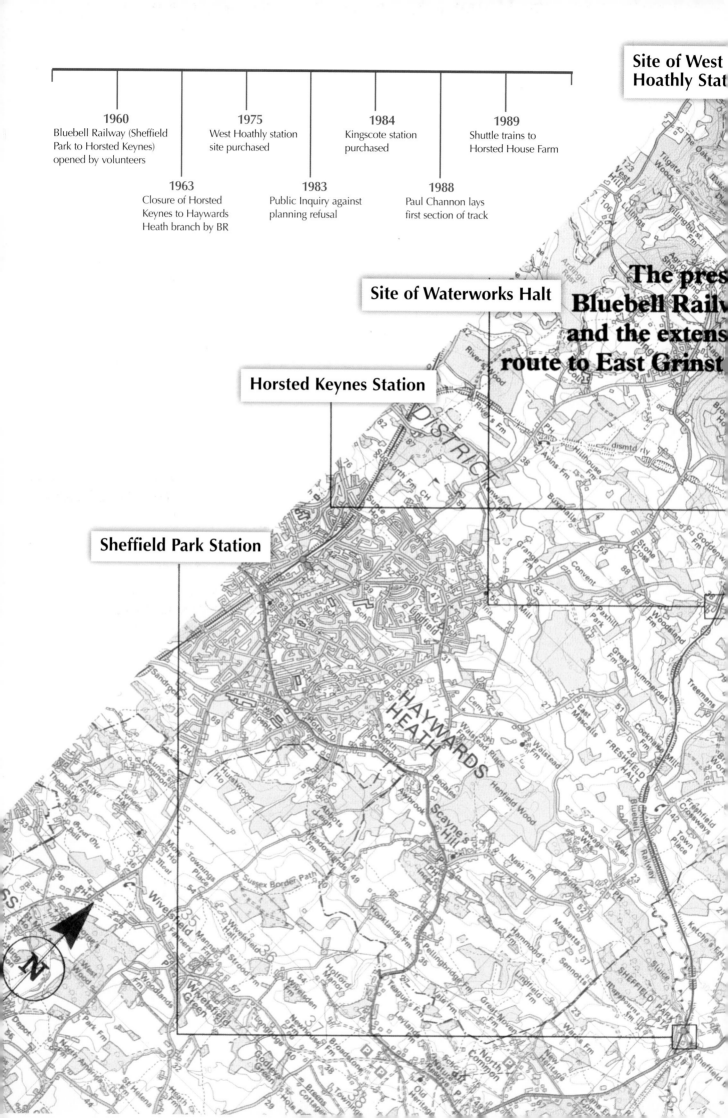

Site of West Hoathly Stat

1960
Bluebell Railway (Sheffield Park to Horsted Keynes) opened by volunteers

1963
Closure of Horsted Keynes to Haywards Heath branch by BR

1975
West Hoathly station site purchased

1983
Public Inquiry against planning refusal

1984
Kingscote station purchased

1988
Paul Channon lays first section of track

1989
Shuttle trains to Horsted House Farm

**The pres
Bluebell Railw
and the extens
route to East Grinst**

Site of Waterworks Halt

Horsted Keynes Station

Sheffield Park Station

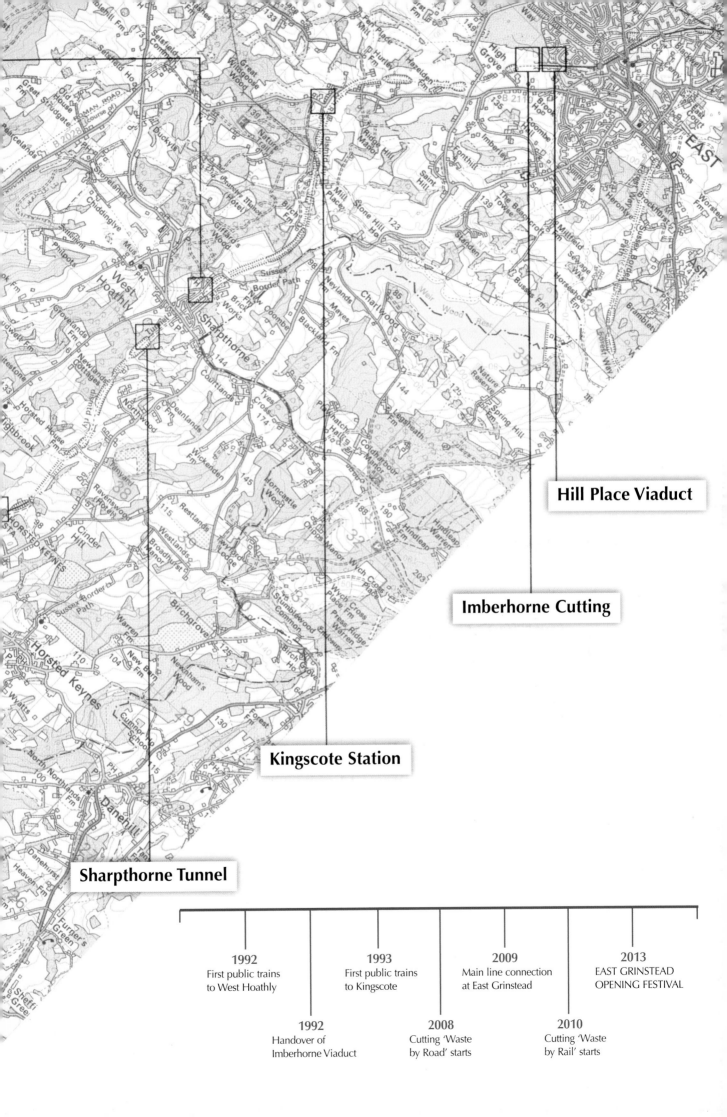

Hill Place Viaduct

Imberhorne Cutting

Kingscote Station

Sharpthorne Tunnel

1992
First public trains
to West Hoathly

1993
First public trains
to Kingscote

2009
Main line connection
at East Grinstead

2013
EAST GRINSTEAD
OPENING FESTIVAL

1992
Handover of
Imberhorne Viaduct

2008
Cutting 'Waste
by Road' starts

2010
Cutting 'Waste
by Rail' starts

North or West – Which is Best?

by Chris Cooper

(A tongue-in-cheek view of the extension saga, first published Bluebell News Summer 1975)

EXPEDITION 1: A PERSONAL VIEW

The current ups and downs in the saga of the proposed extensions and the letters which seem to flow to *Bluebell News*, have reached such momentum that I feel I must put pen to paper, nose to the grindstone and power to the elbow to enlighten my fellow members as to what is involved in six miles one way or two miles the other.

The Northward extension starts just the other side of the Leamland overbridge and about 50 yards further on you will come to a barbed wire fence across the trackbed. Be very careful if you intend to jump this. The trackbed now continues through thick undergrowth to emerge about 100 yards as a farm track right up to Horsted House Farm. The bridge here has been bricked up to provide butts for a rifle range and the scrub on the cutting sides has been cleared. Continue on, using the rubber boat you brought with you, to the tunnel portal where you must unfold your umbrella. The rain outside was nothing compared with what is coming down inside.

Outside the north portal is an assortment of spares for old cars, complete with a rusting Ford Anglia body which was surely 'ripe for preservation'.

The bar of the Bluebell Inn emptied as I arrived and I was able to study the site of West Hoathly station. Part of the platforms survive and I watched two young archaeologists, one of whom appeared to be armour-plated, taking photos of the coping stones. Pursuing a northerly course and noting a sheer drop where the bridge at Coombe had been partially demolished, I picked myself up out of the mud and eventually arrived via waterlogged trackbed at the intact house at Kingscote where I was greeted by a sign 'Trespassers will be shot, and stray dogs prosecuted'. A black and white stuffed tiger in a window was the only thing that eyed my passing however, and further on, rounding the bend, I found to my amazement that someone had very selfishly left a mountain across the line at Imberhorne. The mountain appeared to belong to East Grinstead Council and was volcanic, as a constant flow of old tin cans and bottles was coming from the top.

As the only way round was to remove it or build a rack railway, Swiss-style, I tied a handkerchief round my nose and soon arrived via the viaduct at the buffer stops of British Rail at East Grinstead, whereupon I was charged excess fare from Horsted Keynes on trying to leave the station.

Looking west: the remains of the abutments of Sheriff Mill Viaduct, just west of Horsted Keynes, which was demolished upon closure of the route from Haywards Heath via Ardingly to Horsted Keynes. **MIKE ESAU**

Sharing the success: owning a piece of th

Share issue prospectuses from Bluebell Railway plc from the issues of 1986, 1991 and 2008.

In order to undertake some serious fundraising for the northern extension, Bluebell Railway plc was formed from Bluebell Railway Operating Ltd in 1985, allowing for the first 'offer to subscribe for shares' in the company a year later, in 1986.

Launched amid much fanfare, the issue soon reached its minimum subscription of £100,000 by the deadline of 22 April 1986 and closed at £461,630.

This success enabled further land purchases to be negotiated. On 19 September 1987 it was announced that the railway had obtained two plots of land either side of its present site at Kingscote and in November 1987 came the breakthrough – to obtain the trackbed immediately north of Bluebell's land at Horsted Keynes.

The second share issue in 1991, and

EXPEDITION 2: GO WEST YOUNG MAN

For the trek to Ardingly I decided that I should need better equipment so I purchased a pair of Wellington boots.

The viaduct at Sheriff Mill had been demolished and my 40ft descent was into soft earth, which some would feel was unfortunate. Crossing the lane and dodging a Land Rover I started up the other side. At this point a gentleman stopped and asked me why I was climbing up the wall of the demolished viaduct. My reply was the now famous: "Because it isn't there!"

I proceeded toward the tunnel at Lywood, a tunnel much drier than that at Sharpthorne and progress was much easier, except that a bridge had been removed near Ardingly.

My two and a half mile expedition was nearly at an end for I reached the roadstone plant at Ardingly about 3.30pm. The platform buildings have been swept away but an armless signal remains and it took me some time to decide if I should enter the station. The goods line terminates about 100 yards to the north of the station site and to join up with the BR line would involve moving about 400 tons of stones.

SERIOUS ENDING

To look at both alternatives in a less flippant attitude, it is clear to me that Ardingly would be cheaper if landowners would agree to sell and we could re-bridge two gaps. The disadvantages are that BR probably wouldn't allow us into Haywards Heath and therefore the East Grinstead direction would provide a direct run with no need to reverse and the possibility of an interchange at East Grinstead.

The disadvantages are the length of line, a 700-yard wet tunnel and a huge tip which seems to grow every week. The whole thing on which schemes depend is money and in this direction the drum has been beaten so often that some people are getting fed up with the whole thing. Already a railway revival scheme in Hampshire wants £750,000, to quote the railway press, and all the members of Steam Lines South East want support.

I therefore feel that we should pursue the two and a half mile link to Ardingly as a more viable and direct route to the outside world.

The revised layout at the Amey Roadstone plant at Ardingly, looking east, in 1974. CHRIS COOPER

Author Chris Cooper (right) is typical of a long-term Bluebell volunteer, only recently 'hanging up his hat' after more than four decades of keeping the railway's carriages clean. BRIAN STEPHENSON

luebell Railway

extended by the board to be offered until December 1993, was primarily used for continuing construction of the railway beyond New Coombe Bridge and on to Kingscote station.

The last 'offer for sale of shares' was made in 2008 against a very different financial background than that of the first issue of 1986. The railway had reached Kingscote in April 1994 and had laid track up to Imberhorne Cutting as an engineers' siding. The completion of the last two miles and its 'problem cutting' formed the basis of publicity for the offer and although the so-called 'credit crunch' had started in August 2007 and spare money had begun to get tighter for many people, the railway was still left with a creditable £700,000 of shares purchased by members and well-wishers at the closure of the offer.

An example of press advertising for the 2008 share offer, 'We've got a tip for you'.

The Planning Applications

by Mike Grant

Extension
committee member

The management committee of the Bluebell Railway Preservation Society first gave serious consideration to the possibility of extending the railway north of Horsted Keynes when, in the latter part of 1972, the then owner of Horsted House Farm indicated his willingness to sell the trackbed which extended through his property for some five eighths of a mile. Accordingly, negotiations commenced, planning permission was obtained and Bluebell Railway Ltd launched a Northern Extension Appeal which invited members and friends to donate or lend money for the project.

Regrettably the company was unable to acquire the land as the farm was sold in its entirety and the next owner resisted attempts to re-open negotiations for purchase. From this initial plan grew a body of opinion that the railway ought to make a serious attempt to purchase the land and relay track over the whole six mile stretch between Horsted Keynes and East Grinstead.

West Sussex County Council supported the scheme but advised that a planning application for the West Hoathly station site was pending which would allow housing development to block the route of the projected railway.

A minor breakthrough came in the autumn of 1975 when the railway was able to agree the purchase price of the West Hoathly site at £25,000, somewhat less than anticipated and the vendors agreed to a 90% mortgage for 12 months to allow the railway to continue fundraising.

A detailed feasibility study was presented to Mid Sussex District Council in November 1975 and formed the basis of an application for planning permission for the trackbed between the Horsted House Farm boundary and the northern limit of the West Hoathly site. This application was considered at the meeting of the Development Services Committee on 7 January 1976 and approved, subject to confirmation by MSDC Co-ordinating Committee (i.e. the joint committee of the District and County Councils). At the meeting of the latter committee on 21 January, confirmation was rejected by three votes to two with two abstentions, it being considered that "the farming and forestry usage of the land must take priority over railway usage for primarily leisure purposes and as an access route by adjoining landowners."

The Battle for Bluebell had just begun…

HO/39/78 – CONSTRUCTION OF A RAILWAY BETWEEN HORSTED KEYNES STATION AND EAST GRINSTEAD STATION

The Bluebell Railway Company
TQ 373296 – TQ 388382
Extracts from the report of the District Planning Officer at Mid Sussex District Council, Haywards Heath.

The application related to a proposal to extend the Bluebell Railway from its present northern terminus at Horsted Keynes to connect with the British Rail network at East Grinstead. The length of the proposed line is about five and a half miles and use would be made of the trackbed, its bridges, cuttings and embankments, which still remain for the most part. The line will be single track only with no intermediate stopping places between Horsted Keynes and East Grinstead. Kingscote station will not therefore be used.

With the first planning applications, having either expired or failed, it was time to rethink. With West Hoathly station site in Bluebell ownership and being able to see that there was considerable support, particularly in Horsted Keynes for the railway to be taken through to East Grinstead, thoughts were that it should be pursued. A further planning application (HO/39/78) was therefore prepared and submitted in 1978 for a railway from Horsted Keynes to East Grinstead.

In May 1978, an application was received by Mid Sussex for tipping in the former railway cutting to the south-west of Imberhorne Lane, East Grinstead. (Reference GR/118/78). This application was considered by the Development Services Committee on 19 September 1978, when it was resolved that the Planning Co-ordinating Committee be recommended to refuse permission for the reason that the proposal would be prejudicial to the construction of the extended Bluebell Line. The Planning Co-ordinating Committee, in view of the recommendation from the County Council's Coast and Countryside Committee that the line should be safeguarded, deferred a decision on the application. The applicants have since appealed to the Secretary of State against the failure of the planning authorities to determine their application.

Once the new planning application had been submitted the following processes were carried out by Mid Sussex District Council Planning Department.

Site Appraisal

A thorough site appraisal was carried out inspecting the whole route from Horsted Keynes to East Grinstead. In general it was noted that several lengths of the line were used for farm access but several other sections have become overgrown. At the southern end a cutting was used as a rifle range on a temporary permission that expired in 1981 (HK/3/74), following which the track bed was cleared and formed a well used farm access, uniting the two parts of Horsted House Farm.

Consultation

Parish and Town Councils –
Horsted Keynes Parish Council "As you know, complete opposition has been voiced by the farming community in the area, and my committee is not unanimous in this matter. However, it is generally felt that the application should not be objected to, but there is some opposition to the use of compulsory purchase powers for the purpose."

THE BLUEBELL RAILWAY

ANNOUNCES ITS INTENTION

TO EXTEND ITS PRESENT LINE THROUGH TO EAST GRINSTEAD

The time available for raising funds has been extended to October

WE NEED YOUR SUPPORT NOW

in this exciting venture which will significantly improve leisure facilities in this area

DONATIONS ARE URGENTLY NEEDED

A band of volunteers and staff have kept steam alive in Sussex for the enjoyment of many for 19 years

WILL YOU ADD YOUR EFFORT TO OURS ?

See our Brochure for details or contact:
Bluebell Railway, Sheffield Park, Uckfield, East Sussex
Tel. Newick 2370

PRINTED BY ROGATE PRINTERS, 151 SOUTH STREET, LANCING TEL: 4863 & 4326

A poster announcing the railway's firm intentions, published at the time of the extended mortgage on the West Hoathly site in 1975.

The road to the north: Leamland Bridge at the north end of Horsted Keynes was the limit of Bluebell owned trackbed for many years, seen in 1973. CHRIS COOPER

Compulsory Powers were taken into consideration later by Bluebell in the Light Railway Order application.

West Hoathly Parish Council "Recommend refusal on the grounds that approval would create conditions in Sharpthorne which would be detrimental to the amenity and character of the Hamsey Road/Marlpit Road residential district. The whole of the development of the estate in the past 10 to 20 years depended, to a significant extent, on the fact that the railway no longer existed. Some development had taken place in the close proximity to the tunnel and near the smoke chimneys (ventilator shafts) there, and the owners of such properties would suffer unduly. The proposal to develop the railway line is unquestionably of long term and the immediate development stage of a station at Sharpthorne would also create traffic hazards of considerable and unacceptable magnitude – all traffic to the station having to use the same road for access and exit, and parking space is hopelessly inadequate. Traffic, which from observations would be likely to amount to some 800 vehicles movements per day, would further worsen the problems at the junction of Station Road and Sharpthorne Top Road, which was recently the subject of traffic police investigations. The Parish Council is totally opposed to a 'temporary terminus' at Sharpthorne – it being likely that this could be in operation for many years. Additionally, no thought appears to be given to:

1. the need to clear the many thousands of tons of refuse which has been dumped in the cutting at Imberhorne Lane:

2. the provision of a rail crossing across the proposed East Grinstead bypass."

East Grinstead Town Council "Would support approval subject to:

(a) adequate compensation being provided to the adjoining agricultural land owners, and satisfactory access to their properties being provided by Bluebell Extension Railway Ltd.

(b) adequate precautions for clearing the rubbish to High Grove Tip being made in consultation with a professional body such as the Public Health Authority: and

(c) a reasonable completion date being agreed with the Planning Authority."

The District Planning Officer, Wealden District Council "I would inform you that the Area Plan North Sub-Committee at its meeting on 31 May 1979 resolved to advise you that this Council strongly supports the proposal".

East Sussex County Council. The County Planning Officer has stated – "It is my view that the proposed extension of the Bluebell Railway, as an important improvement to an existing major leisure facility, should be supported. It will enable a vital link to be made with the main line railway which should help to attract more tourists and also improve access to the railway.

The operators have proved their ability to run this major tourist attraction responsibly and in a well organised manner.

Coupled with neighbouring Sheffield Park Gardens, this facility fulfils an extremely important tourist function and this proposal will mean increased prosperity to the county.

The Forestry Commission. Concerned because of a danger of fire. Some timber is subject to a dedication agreement. Safeguarding of timber haulage routes.

British Rail supports the project on commercial grounds because of the revenue benefits which a direct interchange at East Grinstead would give.

Ministry of Agriculture Fisheries and Food

Not opposed subject to conditions that –

(a) Access is maintained;

(b) Adequate fencing is maintained;

(c) Minimise fire risk to adjoining land;

(d) Refuse from High Grove is contained and fenced.

The County Surveyor

No objection is raised provided suitable conditions are imposed with regard to safety of bridges; the protection of the public rights of way; and the removal of waste from High Grove Tip.

Representations from Government and other National Bodies

(i) The National Farmer's Union and the Country Landowners' Association support their members in opposition to the proposal.

(ii) The South East of England Tourist Board supports the application, mentioning the regional significance of the railway and the increasing number of overseas visitors who travel on it.

(iii) The Countryside Commission has indicated that they would not oppose the application.

Representations

118 letters of representations have been received since 1975 on the subject of the proposed extension.

62 of the letters received have expressed an objection to the proposal although some are duplicated. Some related to compulsory purchase objections and do not relate to the use of the land. Points against mainly relate to agriculture and are mostly from those with an interest in the land forming part of the trackbed. Others relate to the rifle range, increased traffic in West Hoathly and disturbance to the occupants of houses near to the line.

There have been 46 letters of support, mainly regarding recreation and enjoyment and perceived transportation benefits which would be obtained from the proposed extension.

County Policy Considerations

The proposal would not conflict with Structural Plan Polices.

County Coast and Countryside Committee

"The proposal has recreational advantages which merit support by permitting, subject to conditions, the application for the extension and by safeguarding the trackbed from other development."

(c) The Coast and Countryside Committee decision was ratified by the County Council in April 1979.

6.Powers of Compulsory Purchase. Light Railway Acts 1896-1912 (Sections 2-14) (Saved by Section 131 Local Government Act 1972)

The above provisions enable a railway company (and indeed local authorities) to apply to The Light railway Commissioners (now the Secretary of State) for an order authorising the light railway pursuant to Section 2 Light Railways Act 1896. Before granting any application for such an order the Secretary of State would first hold a local enquiry into the proposal in order to "give full opportunity for any objections to the to the application to be laid" before him before deciding on the application. The Secretary of State would also need to be satisfied that the planning application for the proposal had been granted.

(See The Light Railway Order, page 26)

7.The categories of Objections

The proposal has attracted a great deal of support as well as considerable localised opposition.

The Committee may find it of assistance to their consideration of the application if the objections are divided into the following categories.
(a)Landowner objections to possible compulsory purchase.
(b)Agricultural and Forestry objections.
(c)Amenity objections.

8. District Council Observations on:

(a) Objections from Landowners

With one, or possibly two exceptions, it would appear, at the time of writing, that all the landowners object to the proposal and have intimated that they are not prepared to sell their land. They object strongly to the possibility of compulsory acquisition at some future date and feel that the proposal is placing a blight over their properties.

Observation:

The objections are understandable but they are not, in themselves valid planning objections.

(b)Agricultural and Forestry Objections

These objections relate to the severance of farms and woodlands, to the danger of fire and to the resultant disruption which, in the opinion of some of the farmers and other landowners, would result from the reopening of the line.

Observation:

It is considered that these potential problems carry great weight in the consideration of the application and for this reason meetings and discussions have been held with farmers and their representatives, together with the applicants to see whether any of their objections can be overcome.

The agricultural objections were also discussed at a meeting attended by representatives of the Railway Company, National Farmers Union, the chairman of the County Planning Committee and your chairman on 29 May 1979 when it was agreed that a further meeting would be held on 25 June with the Railway Company, Individual farm owners together with their respective committee chairman and officers in order to attempt to isolate and resolve the objections of individual farmers.

The outcome of this meeting will be reported verbally.

The Railway Company's approach to severance

The railway company has said that they would deal with these problems in the following ways. Farm tracks, parallel to the railway and within the railway boundary, farm crossings and timber extraction routes would be provided where required. The Railway Company would be responsible for the repayment of grant to the Forestry Commission as a result of a determination of a Dedication Agreement on any timber, and would meet the cost of any rerouting of farm drainage systems. It would enter into management agreements, undertakings to keep rabbits and weeds under control. The company considers that with the line in use and with regular maintenance of the fencing the amount of trespass would be reduced rather than increased.

The Fire Situation

In respect to the problem of fire, the county fire officer has indicated that

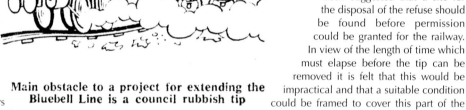

Main obstacle to a project for extending the Bluebell Line is a council rubbish tip

no calls were received as a result of fires alongside the existing Bluebell Line in 1977 and 1978 and only three in 1975. Twelve calls were received in 1976, but that was an unduly dry summer when there was a considerable risk of fire throughout the countryside. The Railway Company has a fire train equipped with two tank wagons of water stationed at Horsted Keynes, but would use diesel engines hired from British Rail, once connection had been made with East Grinstead, in the event of a long dry spell of weather.

(c) Amenity Objections

Observations:

The objections relate to noise, traffic and other disturbances and also to the removal of High Grove Tip. As far as the question of the effect of the railway on individual properties is concerned it is considered that with a few exceptions, particularly at Kingscote, amenities of residential properties close to the line would not be adversely affected to any appreciable extent. The West Hoathly Parish Council has objected strongly to the volume of additional traffic which they fear the railway would generate. It is not proposed, however, to construct a station at Sharpthorne. The only additional traffic would therefore arise from sightseers, it is impossible to forecast the amount of traffic but it would certainly be far less than the volume which could be expected if the line was to terminate at Sharpthorne as was envisaged in the previous application. With regard to High Grove Tip, the County Surveyor has stated that material could not be removed until it had become inert, that is to say in about 15 years time. The removal of the material would need to be carefully controlled but it is felt that adequate conditions could be imposed to safeguard this. It had originally been suggested that a site for the disposal of the refuse should be found before permission could be granted for the railway. In view of the length of time which must elapse before the tip can be removed it is felt that this would be impractical and that a suitable condition could be framed to cover this part of the development.

9.Conclusions

The proposal is extremely ambitious for a voluntary body.

The Railway Company has suggested that the period required for the completion of the scheme may be 30 years or more. It also estimates that it would have to meet costs of £1 million.

The proposal accords with county policy and has the support of the Coast and Countryside Committee. It therefore falls to this committee to consider the local; implications and objections and to weigh them against the desirable strategic planning objectives embodied in County Policy.

RECOMMENDATION OF THE DEVELOPMENT SERVICES COMMITTEE

That permission be refused for the following reasons:
1.The proposal would be detrimental to the proper management of agriculture and forestry in this predominantly rural area.
2.The proposal would, by virtue of the generation of traffic noise and a general increase in the level of activity, detract from the amenities of this attractive rural area and from the peace and harmony to which the residents of the area might reasonably expect to be entitled.

The Bluebell Trustees, having received the refusal notice approached the membership of the Preservation Society to ask for any of its members with professional skill in planning, surveying and engineering, the law, accountancy and any other associated professions if they would be able to give their time to serve on an Extension Committee with the view of preparing to make an appeal against the refusal to grant the planning permission.

The Bluebell Extension Railway Limited had already been formed and registered in September 1975 to be the vehicle to handle the planning and construction of the Extension Railway to East Grinstead.

Above: Much of the planning correspondence of the 1970s and 1980s made reference to the 'amenity tip' at High Grove (Imberhorne) Cutting and when it was considered safe or practical for the rubbish to be moved. The cutting and its troubles seemed a very, very, long way off in the 1970s. This is the north end of the tip at Hill Place Farm, looking south. MIKE ESAU

Left: 'Branch line': The view looking north of the trackbed at Horsted House Farm. MIKE ESAU

6-MILE LINK FOR BLUEBELL LINE

AS a long-term project, the Bluebell Railway Preservation Society in Sussex is planning to extend to East Grinstead its five-mile-long, privately-run line.

It would add another five to six miles to the vintage railway —from Horsted Keynes to the town's station, via Sharpthorne and Kingscote.

The joint planning, roads and transportation sub-committee of West Sussex County Council is sympathetic to the idea, and is recommending that the coast and countryside committee has a look at the recreational advantages of assisting the society.

The steam railway enthusiasts propose relaying the track on the bed of the former link that wound its way through the blue-

bell woods to the old county town of Lewes until it was axed in the pre-Beeching era.

★

One big obstacle the society would have to overcome is the council - owned High Grove refuse tip and its neighbouring private dump in the deep cutting either side of Imberhorne Lane, at East Grinstead.

Mr William Brophy, chairman and one of the six trustees of the Bluebell Railway Ltd., said yesterday:

"We felt that we should at least make an approach now to the council. No buildings have been put up on the old railway land and it might be possible to make a single cutting rather than a double track hole through the tip.

"Our car parks are filled to

capacity on busy days and this limits the number of visitors. The rail connections at East Grinstead would take traffic off the congested A275 Wych Cross to Lewes road and bring extra custom to British Rail as well as improving our living museum of vintage steam trains."

In addition to a revenue balance of £38,400, the Bluebell Co. has a reserve fund of £33,000. A record number of 252,455 fare-paying passengers were carried on the line in the last year.

FOREST PICNICS

Eight new picnic sites are planned in Sherwood Forest, Notts, by the Forestry Commission.

Daily Telegraph 1975. CHRIS COOPER COLLECTION

The Extension Railway Committee

by Mike Grant

The first meeting of Bluebell Extension Railway Ltd's committee took place on 27 April 1980 at 10am. The Extension Committee consisted of: chairman of the Preservation Society, Terry Cole, acting as chairman of the committee, David Ratcliff – a driver, as vice-chairman, Bernard Holden – The Superintendent of the Line, Nick Stanbury – Secretary of the Bluebell Extension Railway Ltd, and other members of the Preservation Society who had offered their services and had been invited to join the committee, having suitable professional skills to assist in the preparation of an appeal to the refusal of planning permission and in preparing evidence and a Light Railway Order application in connection with it. They were, Ron Potter (RP) – a planning expert with the London Borough of Hillingdon with specific experience in moving refuse tips for building the M25 motorway; Raymond Duthoit – a lawyer; Robin Higgs – chairman Mid-Hants Railway with particular experience in planning and constructing private railway extensions for both Mid-Hants and Welsh Highland Railways; Alan Broderick – a civil engineer and myself, Mike Grant, – a surveyor. Also Tony Sullivan – a surveyor and member of the BRPS and David Wallis – employed by BR Southern Region at Croydon, experienced in signalling, and also a member of the BRPS committee.

Planning matters generally were discussed. Ayling & Strudwick, Bluebell's surveyors, who submitted the planning application, reported that a joint planning enquiry with the Rookery estates appeal – application GR/118/78 for tipping south of Imberhorne Lane Bridge – was possible; it was not considered whether any objection was appropriate. It would be necessary to appoint suitable experts to deal with agricultural and forestry objections.

A Light Railway Order (LRO) and constructional matters were discussed in detail – in the light of drafts supplied by solicitors the need to appoint a supervising engineer. It was agreed that Alan Broderick be appointed for the time being. Bernard Holden and I were to pursue detailed requirements for the book of reference before a meeting could be arranged with the solicitor.

At the next meeting held on 8 June, five members of the committee were selected to meet the Parliamentary Agents. Peter Thomas was appointed minutes secretary. On 13 July Terry Cole asked to be relieved of his position as chairman due to other workload. This was accepted and he was thanked for his considerable services in the chair since the formation of the company. David Ratcliff was appointed in his place and Alan Broderick was appointed a director of the company. A draft application for an LRO was received from the solicitor who said that it was not known when the appeal would be heard.

Kingscote lost

It was understood that Kingscote station had unexpectedly come on to the market for about £60,000 and should be seriously considered.

On 21 September Kingscote station house had been inspected and found to be in reasonable condition, although some work would be necessary. It would be needed as a base station for the northward extension, and also as a temporary terminus until a way through the tip to East Grinstead could be carried out. On 12 October a sold notice had been placed at Kingscote and that offers considerably in excess of Bluebell's offer had been made. The agents were to be contacted. On 2 November it was confirmed that Kingscote had been sold for a sum of £62,500 to a local man.

At this time, an estimate had been made of the approximate cost of building the railway and what funds would be required to finance it. A figure of £2,100,000 was mentioned but it is not thought that this included the removal of the Tip at Imberhorne Lane Cutting which had not been assessed at that time – although an approximate estimate of clearing the cutting could be in the region of £4m to £5m. A visit to a landfill site in Buckinghamshire and also the Crowhurst Brickworks site, adjacent to the railway near Lingfield, was made and plans were made on the basis that the refuse would be removed by rail as road haulage would be very expensive and have to go through the East Grinstead area which was not advisable. Very few properties were able to be visited at the time and until they could be, positive discussions with the owners could not take place. The various plots of land involved amounted to 30, so it would not be possible to cost the work accurately.

PREPARING FOR THE PUBLIC INQUIRY

Work on researching information and evidence for the public inquiry was now going ahead. I had been appointed to prepare drawings for the LRO application but information was not easy to obtain due to properties not being accessible and technical details of the infrastructure not being to hand but a set of preliminary drawings could be completed – see The Light Railway Order (LRO) page 26.

At a meeting with counsel in December 1980 concern was raised regarding the LRO and that drawings could not be completed early enough to set a date for the inquiry. The drawings had to be deposited at least three months in advance. At any rate insufficient information was available for the drawings to be progressed. Counsel felt that it might be

Kingscote Station, waiting for trains again in 1983. BOB BAMBEROUGH

Prior to demolition and tracklifting, the scene at West Hoathly station looking south towards the tunnel, on 15 June 1963. LESLIE SANDLER/ *RAILWAY MAGAZINE*

very difficult to obtain the necessary Compulsory Purchase Orders (CPOs) for what is in effect a leisure activity. It could be that obtaining CPOs was not really practicable, and that the LRO should be separated from the planning appeal. This could result in objections being withdrawn or diminished if planning approval was given.

On 18 January 1981 an offer was received from a retired railway engineer to assist. Also Bill Nobes, a BR Southern Region bridge engineer, would also be available. This offer proved crucial, as will be seen later. A rumour that Horsted House Farm had been sold proved to be correct. This also opened up new possibilities and investigations were to be carried out.

Raymond Duthoit had met the new owner of Kingscote station, a Greek gentleman, whereby matters of mutual interest had been satisfactorily discussed.

I had received a letter which gave a contact for an agricultural and forestry expert. I investigated it further. Preliminary plans for the LRO were nearly ready.

On 22 February 1981 a letter was received from the DOE at Bristol saying that they would not be prepared to grant an indefinite adjournment. A firm date of 23 June 1981 had been offered at East Grinstead that was subsequently postponed. The Parliamentary Agents felt optimistic about an LRO provided that CPOs were not included. The preliminary LRO preparation was all but ready, although

insufficient information was available to complete them. The directors of the Extension Company decided that approaches should be made to all landowners as soon as possible.

I was meeting Professor Wibberley of University College London, my agricultural and forestry expert in London, on 5 March. At that meeting we were provided with a contact, Roger Sayce, a Chartered Rural Practice Surveyor, who had set up the firm Rural Planning Services Ltd at Didcot. He and other colleagues considered environmental matters and were currently looking at the Stansted Airport proposal. The Bluebell extension was not so complicated. Ron Potter and I were able to go to Didcot and meet him. By 22 March I had met with Rural Planning Services Ltd, who were able to assist and were optimistic in rebutting reasons for the planning refusal. The company asked them to act, provided they could prepare the report in time for the inquiry. I would assist the planners to reduce cost and save time.

On 22 May after counsel had seen the drafts of the evidence, each of the main properties were considered separately.

1. The Rifle Range – if planning permission was not renewed it could be discounted. Horsed House Farm, of which the rifle range was part, had not been included.
2. Timber Extraction – a) review the access; b) alternative methods of extraction; c) the dedication agreement.

3. The Tunnel – a written agreement from BR to sell, or arrange evidence for the inquiry.
4. West Hoathly station – consider possible sightseers causing nuisance to the neighbourhood.
5. New Coombe Farm – seek confirmatory letter from the owner of his agreement to the extension.
6. Birch Farm Nursery – can alternative land be found to accommodate his planting beds presently on the trackbed?
7. Two underbridges north of Mill Place Farm – in use. Mill Place Farm did not appear to be included in this review.
8. Kingscote station – examine the possible amenity objections of a railway close to the house and also other properties in the neighbourhood.
9. Ash Lea Farm – provision of an underpass.
10. Kingscote House – examine possible amenity objections.
Other properties adjacent between Vowels Lane Bridge and Hazelden Farm (Rookery Estates) had not been included.
11. Rookery Estates – application for tipping and the appeal against planning for it to be checked upon.
12. Imberhorne Tip – insert period before removal was possible, obtain dates on similar open tips. Hill Place Farm, adjacent to the north end of the tip, had not been included.
13. The Viaduct – discuss value with BR.
14. East Grinstead – discuss outline finance with BR.

By June 1981 further approaches had been made to owners of properties adjacent to the trackbed – most of whom owned sections of it adjacent to their land. In some cases it proved fruitful and in some it did not. This eventually resulted in the railway being able to purchase half of an embankment or cutting, particularly north of Kingscote, but in the end it did give a route through using a single line only but this was satisfactory.

Also in June, Graham Flight, an East Grinstead based chartered accountant, had been contacted and had agreed to join the committee. This now made a difference to the committee as an expert in finance could be included.

A meeting with the Department of Transport at its Marsham Street offices had taken place and a number of points relating to the rules associated with the LRO were raised. It was this meeting that helped considerably to open up opportunities for resolving many issues. No date had yet been put forward for the planning appeal.

A letter was received by the solicitor from the DOE at Bristol dated 19 October 1982 saying that the appeal hearing could not be delayed indefinitely and suggested that if the problems relating to evidence and the LRO could not be resolved shortly that the appeal should be withdrawn and a fresh application might be made. The company was not prepared to withdraw the appeal against the planning decision of 1979. The solicitor replied accordingly but it did put pressure on Bluebell to resolve matters as soon as possible.

In November a meeting was held with BR when it was asked if it could withdraw its holding objections – that was agreed to and that a lease of the East Grinstead site could be agreed. When electrification of the line was completed the up siding need not be required so Bluebell could adjust its plans for its station accordingly.

In December I advised that I had completed the LRO drawings and incorporated all the recent amendments. It had been submitted to the parliamentary agents for putting on deposit on 1 January 1983. Agreement had been reached with Southbridge Building Supplies in connection with Kingscote goods yard area required by the company. Agreements had been established on 39½% of the route miles required. If an agreement was reached over Hazelden Farm the figure would reach 47%. Discussions with other land owners would be progressed as events occurred and access was established.

In January it appeared that Mid Sussex District Council had not fully dealt with the publicity matters and the reasons for refusal. Action was being closely monitored. The Central Electricity Generating Board, Seeboard, Segas and Southern Water all advised that should there be any re-location or diversion of their services as a result of relaying the railway, the company would pay the reasonable costs incurred. This could enable holding objections from utility companies to be withdrawn.

In February a letter from Mid Sussex District Council gave the details of the council's objections and refusal of planning permission. The solicitor was now able to write to the DOE in Bristol suggesting that the public inquiry would be held in May-June 1983. It was important that a date was agreed so that society members could be advised at their AGM in late March.

In early March, a date for the inquiry had not yet been received but by April the date of commencement was to be Tuesday 21 June at the offices of The Mid Sussex District Council in Haywards Heath. On 12 May surveys were updated on as many properties as possible.

1. Hill Place Farm – objections are environmental regarding the Tip but it was believed that any farming objections could be overcome.
2. Mill Place Farm – the owner was standing by his fellow farmers. An issue regarding a water pipe could be resolved.
3. Ingwersen Nurseries – to be seen on 1 June.
4. Ash Lea Farm – A first visit. RPS believed that any farming objection could be overcome.
5. Highbrook Estate – not officially surveyed but it was hoped to visit on 1 June.
6. Coombe Place Farm – an option to purchase draft has been sent. Bridge Design had been agreed and an access road could be provided. It had been decided that CPOs would not be included in the LRO.

RPS was nearly ready to approach formally the NFU to ask for collective objections to be removed and to make collective general discussions available with all the farmers on the route. Their report was received by 12 June and approved.

A final option agreement for New Coombe Farm was forwarded. When it had been agreed and signed RPS could contact Ingwersen's to discuss the transfer of land purchased from New Coombe Farm so that their objection could be removed.

The resulting Public Inquiry was to take place in Haywards Heath from 21 June 1983. David Ratcliffe asked Horsted Keynes station staff Paul Ritchie and Alan Fell to unroll a large banner at the 26 March Bluebell AGM. "Share my faith in the future" David challenged the membership. The inquiry took 10 full days of sittings over three weeks and Lord Broxbourne QC represented the Bluebell Railway.

The Bluebell Railway

Help our Planning Appeal
to relay the track between
Horsted Keynes and East Grinstead.

Join a SPONSORED WALK – Saturday 5th JUNE 1982

While waiting for the public inquiry to its planning appeal, the railway continued its popular sponsored walks in June and October 1982, to help defray the anticipated costs of professional representation and advice at the hearing.

Bluebell extension plan runs into trouble at Sharpthorne

Although the Bluebell Railway authorities say they are making good progress in their negotiations to buy the site of the old West Hoathly railway station—a key step in their bid to extend the line from Horsted Keynes to East Grinstead stations—other landowners are refusing to part with the land on which the railway track used to run.

Mrs. C. P. Wykeham-Martin, on whose Horsted House Farm, near Sharpthorne, lies a vital half-mile of former railway track, linking up with the boundary of the Blue-bell railway line."

said, "and he has entered into a covenant with the Forestry Commission that the length of old track he owns shall be used only for forestry and agriculture—not for a railway line."

the purchase of the West Hoathly station site and everything seems to be going satisfactorily in that direction. The target is £60,000."

Its purchase was vital to the success of the scheme and there was some urgency in the matter, for the present owners had put in an application for housing development on the site.

"If we should not be able to clinch the West Hoathly purchase," Mr. Holden said, "all the money subscribed will be refunded allocated to some other scheme

in accordance with the wishes of each individual subscriber."

Mr. Holden added that the proposed re-opening of the line was a long-term project and could involve up to 15 years. "If we go ahead," he said, "we shall try to buy the necessary land from the new owners by agreement.

"The whole situation could be vastly different in 15 years' time and as far as the Bluebell Line is concerned at present the suggestion is not

The closed station at Kingscote on 15 June 1963. The British Railways enamel signboard was later removed by an enthusiast but donated back when the Bluebell arrived and it is now exactly in the same position at the restored station. LESLIE SANDLER/ RAILWAY MAGAZINE

The Light Railway Order (LRO)

by Mike Grant

The Light Railways Act of 1896 was introduced to help in the construction of railways in rural areas and a Light Railway Order that included compulsory purchase powers could be obtained to build and operate them.

An LRO was suggested as most appropriate for the construction of the Bluebell's extension to East Grinstead but it contained many requirements and information to be submitted to obtain it. While Bluebell's solicitor handled the actual application, I was appointed the task of preparing a set of drawings to show what was being proposed and where it would go. These drawings had to include the following information:

1. A plan showing the route to be followed and the properties that it was to go through and where those properties' boundaries were along the line.
2. The extent of land required each side of the line shown as lines of deviation, being the lines that the railway track should be contained within.
3. The actual distance between the start and finish points marked in 100 metre divisions on the plan.
4. A plan showing the gradients of the line from start to finish.
5. Levels shown throughout related to existing OS bench marks at both ends of the line.
6. All culverts, under and over bridges, crossings, footpaths, tunnels and viaducts to be shown with levels of the top of the running line and underside of any overbridge showing clearances, heights of structures, water courses and other access points etc.

It can be seen that the amount of information to be provided was considerable and the drawings had to be prepared in an acceptable format. It was through meetings with the very helpful parliamentary agents in Westminster that I was able to do this. If the line were to be constructed from scratch it would all have had to be surveyed from beginning to end. Fortunately the infrastructure existed almost in its entirety except for New Coombe Bridge that had been removed north of West Hoathly station and of course Imberhorne Cutting that had been filled with domestic refuse and excavations from Beeching Way in East Grinstead.

In addition to this we were not able to get access to many properties to obtain measurements; so I was extremely grateful when Bernard Holden, after a meeting we had at the Department of Transport in Marsham Street, Westminster, put me in touch with Bill Nobes, a bridge engineer at BR. He provided me with a complete set of copies of the original LEGR 1880 construction drawings – showing every bridge, culvert, tunnel and viaduct – with levels shown that gave me the essential information needed for the application. That was a major breakthrough!

> **"Bill Nobes provided me with a complete set of copies of the original LEGR 1880 construction drawings that gave me the essential information needed for the application."**

The hand drawn coloured originals had been kept, together with drawings for every structure on all Southern Railway lines from Broadstairs to Padstow – neatly stowed away in an arch underneath Waterloo station. Without that we would not have been able to obtain an LRO and build the railway as there was an objector ready to take out an injunction to stop us if he had his chance. It was crucial to the success of the whole project. It took time to obtain and include this information but it made all the difference.

Before granting any application for such an order, the Secretary of State would first hold a local inquiry into the proposal in order to "give full opportunity for any objections to the application to be laid before him" before deciding on the application. The Secretary of State would also need to be satisfied that the planning application for the proposal had been granted so both the planning and LRO applications were dependent upon each other. Once the LRO had succeeded, the planning could go forward. The drawings had to be

What the papers said...

Landowners declare battle on rail link

ELEVEN landowners have unanimously agreed to fight the scheme to expand the Bluebell Railway into East Grinstead from Horsted Keynes.

Their decision came after a meeting at the home of Mr Phil Wykeham-Martin, of Sharpthorne. And six other landowners who could not be present sent in letters of objection.

They passed a resolution saying they opposed the scheme because of its "serious detrimental effect on the environment and on agricultural, horticultural and forestry businesses."

The landowners have already said they would not be willing to sell their parts of the line to the Bluebell Railway.

Support for the landowners has come from the National Farmers Union, the Council For the Protection of Rural England, the Country Landowners' Association, the National Smallbore Rifle Association and the Conservators of Ashdown Forest.

The names of the landowners and organisations backing them have been sent to six parish, district and county councils; the British Railways Board; Mid Sussex MP Tim Renton.

Farmers' fears on steam rail plan

Rail buffs' battle runs out of puff

THE VINTAGE steam train buffs who run the Bluebell

TABLE 2: PLOT LOCATIONS AND LENGTHS

Plot	Identification	Approximate location on order plans (in metres)	Approximate lengths of track bed (in metres)			
			A	B	C	D
1	(Bluebell Railway)	0–50	50			
2,3,4	(Hilton Investments)	50–1210				1160
5	(Orpin)	–				
6	(Courtland Wood)	1210–2500				
7	(tunnel)	2500–3125		625		
8	(West Hoathly St.)	3125–3650	525			
9	(Deans)	3650–4350			700	
11	(Ingwersen)	4350–5220				
12	(cattle creep)	5220–5230		10		
13	(Leggat)	5230–5350				)
15	(Leggat)	5360–6130				) 890
14	(bridge)	5350–5360		10		
16	(Moran)	6130–6260			130	
17	(Kingscote St.)	6260–6385	125			
18	(Moran depot)	6385–6645			260	
19	(bridge)	6645–6655		10		
20	(Jones)	6655–6810 East				)
21	(Double)	6810–6910 East				) 255
22	(Bacon)	6655–6910 West				)
23	(bridge)	6910–6920		10		
24	(Foster)	6920–7230 West				)
25	(Omegna)	6920–7130 East				) 310
26	(Steer)	7130–7230 East				)
27	(Harding)	7230–7470				240
28	(May)	7470–8250				780
29	(bridge)	8250–8260		10		
30	(tip and bridge)	8260–8700		440		
31	(Hobbs)	8700–9155				455
32	(viaduct etc)	9155–9880		725		
			700	1840	1090	4090
						3200

A – owned by Bluebell Railway or Bluebell Extension Railway   700 m   7%

B – owned by British Railways or West Sussex County Council   1840 m   19%

C – privately owned on which Bluebell Extension Railway holds options or agreement (see paragraph 11.1)   1090 m   11%

D – owned by objectors, excluding British Railways (ascertained by reference to Documents 10,12,15)   4090 m   41%

E – In negotiation   2160 m   22%

9880

Note: ownerships are based on the agreed Document 4.

The 32 plot locations and lengths for properties affected by the LRO. At this time, Bluebell only owned three plots amounting to 700 metres of track (7%) and British Railways/West Sussex County Council 1840 metres (19%). The rest was in private hands with no guarantee of sale. BLUEBELL ARCHIVE

The two maps that accompanied the original Light Railway Order application. BLUEBELL ARCHIVE

deposited at least three months in advance so this process could take place.

Bernard Holden and I were to pursue detailed requirements for the book of reference. This involved preparing a list of the 30 different owners of the properties affected. This was completed and included with the LRO drawings.

The parliamentary agents felt optimistic about an LRO provided CPOs were not included. It was decided that CPOs would not be included. They finally put the LRO on deposit on January 1, 1983.

Writing in Spring 2010, Chris White says:

"A number of people have asked what legislation is involved in constructing and operating the last phase of the extension now the Light Railway Order process is no more. In practice the railway from Sheffield Park to Kingscote does (and will) continue to operate on the extant Light Railway Orders granted as the railway has moved northwards. Put simply, the last section from Kingscote to East Grinstead is constructed under the 1985 planning permission to extend from Horsted Keynes to East Grinstead while the actual operation will be permitted by issue of a licence from the Office of Rail Regulation – as indeed are all railways now, be they main line or heritage.

"Possession of a licence is essential to operate a public train service and will only be granted when HM Railway Inspector (who is also now part of the Office of Rail Regulation) is satisfied we have correctly constructed the extension in accordance with plans submitted to him in 2008 and have a suitable safety management system in place. This good gentleman visits us regularly to monitor progress. In essence, this describes the basic process involved albeit there is quite a bit of discussion and head scratching involved along the way to make sure everything fits into place and the detail is correct.

"It would be lovely to have the good old days of a Light Railway Order back again – things were much simpler; but like it or not we are faced with much the same legislative requirements as any other railway these days. Dealing with this process and other environmental and planning requirements occupy a good deal of time; but getting ticks in the right boxes is essential to running Bluebell by keeping our insurers and government happy.

Battle for East Grinstead station

When British Rail, in its sub-sector pre-privatisation guise of Network SouthEast, formally handed over Hill Place Viaduct in 1992 for £1, it came with an 'understanding' that BR had reserved some space for a Bluebell station at East Grinstead (as there would be no point in taking on the ownership and maintenance liabilities of the Grade II listed structure if it didn't lead to a station!)

But with rail privatisation and the formation of Railtrack, it seemed that Bluebell's 'one pound grace and favour' station was now worth £750,000 to those with outside commmercial interests.

From Bluebell News Spring 1997.

There has been considerable activity over the past 15 months to protect our future northern terminus. In October 1995, J Sainsbury PLC lodged a planning application for a petrol station on the season ticket holders' car park in front of the present station. The application proposed re-siting the car parking on land designated for the Bluebell station. As to be expected, Bluebell lodged an objection to the application.

The application was subsequently amended, then added to. Some of the amendment related to traffic flows but all versions still showed part of our proposed station as re-sited car parking. A further application, quite separate from the previous one, was lodged in March 1996, showing use of part of our station site. This was the first time Sainsbury's recognised our interest in the station site. Again an objection was lodged.

When the planning authority, Mid Sussex District Council, come to consider the applications, the 1996 application was refused on the grounds that it affected the proposed Bluebell station. The 1995 application, as amended and added to, was adjourned for a meeting to take place between the interested parties to see if difficulties could be resolved. Our position has been that if a suitable arrangement could be found, we would certainly consider it.

Next a meeting was called by Railtrack, together with Bluebell and J Sainsbury representatives, to examine an alternative proposal from track experts engaged by Railtrack. The proposal was considered by our advisers and a special meeting was called to examine the new proposal. The directors agreed how far we could go in negotiations, and whether one platform would meet out trafffic requirements but the alternative proposal was rejected. The main reasons were that the points outside the station would be on the viaduct, the platforms would be above the existing formation, the exchange with BR would be on built-up formation and the likely disturbance to nearby houses would be unacceptable and unlikely to receive planning approval. Also the moving back of the station some 80 metres would be a long walk for our passengers and reduce the presence of our station to an unacceptable level.

The next step was that J Sainsbury appealed to the Secretary of State against refusal by the planning authority. The Bluebell has lodged outline objections should the appeal progress further. This may be simply a protection of its position by J Sainsbury but we must also protect our railway's interests.

The latest is that Railtrack has intimated that it will now exclude the land reserved for the Bluebell from its proposals. We hope that this particular worry is almost over now, though we have to watch that any new proposals do not impinge on access to our future station.

PETER THOMAS

The Bluebell's track layout at East Grinstead, into a single platform with run-round facility and access (left) to Network Rail. Some of the initial plans called for the whole Bluebell operation to be 20 metres further south, which would have meant that there would have been points on the viaduct, something unacceptable to today's rail regulators. ANDREW STRONGITHARM

The draft letter below, undated, by Bernard Holden, relates to concerns over the East Grinstead site and also makes mention of the 80 metres zone.

History

In the early 1970s we secured planning permission for the trackbed to Horsted House Farm and on purchase of the West Hoathly site in 1975 we applied to extend this permission to West Hoathly. West Hoathly Parish Council objected to the application, thence the extension to West Hoathly was refused.

Following advice from several supporting bodies we made application for an extension from Horsted Keynes to East Grinstead because by that time our permission over Horsted House Farm had expired and we were further advised not to include any intermediate stations as this would bring in too many objectors (Kingscote was a private residence):- hence we eventually obtained the Secretary of State's permission and a Light Railway Order for a single line from Horsted Keynes to East Grinstead and hence the site at East Grinstead needed to be of sufficient size for a proper station – with two platforms in view of the length of intermediate section.

The permission was given 'in the national interest' and as time has progressed we now have a crossing station at Kingscote so the situation regarding train working has eased to the original idea, but the traffic levels of the 1980s may or may not return. An hourly service would seem to be the favourite for most operating days and in this case the crossing of the two trains would take place at Horsted Keynes, given a right time operation which may not be strictly feasible because you could not start a train from East Grinstead if a down South Central (SC) train is running in and leaving people 50-odd minutes to wait. If there is a surge of traffic from SC owing to road congestion etc., and then a half an hour service is just possible but very tight but Kingscote may supply a safety valve with a stand-by train.

In any event some amenity such as refreshments and shop etc., is required on our site at East Grinstead so that people are not left 'up in the air' for 20 minutes or so and to give ourselves a proper standing in the town. Steve Johnstone is concerned that having worked so hard for 10 years to get to East Grinstead that we need a proper presence and recognition of the society, company and volunteer efforts.

Following a conversation with Major Poyntz, the Inspector for Preservation Liaison, he asked to see the plans and he would point them in the right direction for someone to come and see us and in the letter to him the following questions were put:

1. Is one buffer stop acceptable although the Railtrack plan shows two as required by R.I.
2. Ease of gradient from the viaduct.
3. Passenger area too small and congested at the point off the SC platform.
4. Emergency appliance access to be agreed with presumably J Sainsbury and Railway Inspectorate.

Railtrack has offered us a ticket office in its booking hall and presumably a section for a shop. While the width of the site may be a fait accompli the loss of 80 metres at the north end is a problem and we need several decisions, largely bound up with what the Railway Inspectorate may say, but one buffer stop will enable 30

metres to be saved on our site and this would draw the pointwork off of the viaduct which Steve considered will be a problem in view of the condition of the first arch of the viaduct on which he is currently working. Major Poyntz considered its work on the viaduct very commendable and the cost of all this should be made known (approximately £90,000 into 1997) and further work has to be done on that first arch at a cost of some £25,000 which will be next year's construction budget, similar to this year.

The main decision to be made is whether we accept the restricted site, or at least request an easement of it. I am told the 57 car parking spaces are regularly booked although I have

noted some spare spaces, or do we maintain our ownership of that 80 metres. In fact our plan shows it as being part of our Light Railway Order and of course we have a Letter of Intent without consideration from BR Property Board whose successors Railtrack have accepted. This is a legal question but it occurs to me there is a possibility of leasing this park to Railtrack for its project for say three years or, as a member suggested, that Sainsbury's put its petrol station in its own car park where there appears to be room. It does not seem that there is going to be a quick answer to Railtrack because we are dependent on the Railway Inspector for his recommendations and we need legal advice regarding the land title.

The highlighted Bluebell land (in yellow) at East Grinstead and its relation to Network Rail (to the left) and Sainsbury's (right). PHILIP LANE PHOTOGRAPHY

From Bluebell News Winter 2002.

As recently reported in front page headlines, the Bluebell v Sainsbury's debacle re-entered the fray. This took us completely by surprise and we were somewhat taken aback at what unfolded. Some members will probably be asking why it has taken so long to have got this far, not having completed the deal, and here we are now potentially fighting a giant with financial muscle. So let's put the facts on the table:

a) The land was promised to Bluebell in exchange for assuming responsibility for the restoration and upkeep of Hill Place Viaduct.

b) Two years ago I reported that our solicitor was in active negotiation with Railtrack to facilitate transfer.

c) Railtrack was happy to progress with the deal.

d) Due to the march of time and a succession of owners, certain 'ownership' problems had to be cleared.

e) We agreed to pay Railtrack's legal fees as part of the deal to conclude.

f) Railtrack went into administration, bringing huge changes to its internal organisation and bringing new personnel and process to the theatre.

g) Having agreed contracts, all the people we were dealing with at Railtrack 'moved on'.

h) We were unaware of Sainsbury's interest as indeed were the local council, who had only visited the site two weeks previous.

We have worked very hard and close with the Office of the Rail Regulator (ORR) in the provision of documentation and information, which we retain.

We must now await the ORR ruling *(which was ultimately positive, Ed)*.

ROY WATTS

THE PUBLIC INQUIRY
Tuesday 21 June 1983
Oaklands, Haywards Heath, West Sussex

by Peter Thomas

It was difficult to believe that the date of the inquiry had at last arrived after so many unavoidable deferments. We arrived at Oaklands with cars full of papers and an atmosphere of tense expectancy – had we covered all the matters which the Council, the objectors and most importantly the Inspector would consider to be vital issues? For some witnesses it was their first experience of the inquiry process, for those with some experience there was the heightened awareness that things could go wrong. The Inspector appointed for the inquiry was Stephen Marks.

The 'railway' in the shape of Bluebell Extension Railway Ltd, (known as the Promoters), was represented by Sir Derek Walker-Smith QC, assisted by Eian Caws as his junior. Mr Martin Wood of Counsel appeared for Mid-Sussex District Council (the council), Messrs Hilton Investments Ltd, and the National Farmers Union. Some of the farmers and landowners also appeared, Mr Hilton, Mr Robson, Mr Ingwersen, Mr Leggat, Mr Foster, Mr Harding, Mr May and Mr Hobbs. There were other persons who indicated a wish to address the Inspector. Mr Holmes an East Grinstead resident, and Mr Wykeham-Martin who wished to speak in opposition. In addition, there were letters against the proposal and over 2000 in support, plus three petitions and the Vintage Sunday survey.

Copies of an option to purchase the trackbed at New Coombe Farm and land adjacent to Messrs Ingwersens, signed that very morning, were handed to the inspector.

Sir Derek, in opening the case for the promoters explained the unusual nature of the inquiry. He told the inspector that the reasons for

refusal of planning permission left out more pertinent facts than they included. There was no reference to the planning advice received, no reference to the consensus of consent and no reference to Council procedures. Quoting liberally from the *Mid-Sussex Times*, he said the council's policies over the matter were bizarre, Gilbertian and bearing the aspects of a Mad Hatter's tea party, as the evidence would show. He made reference to the council's approach to the railway, suggesting a feasibility study for the possible extension, and also to the approval and support from West Sussex County Council.

Referring to the Light Railway Order, he said that the Extension Company was not seeking Compulsory Purchase powers: However, he felt it his duty to explain the position in law to the Inspector. Should one or two landowners seek to hold the promoters to ransom, the law catered for such a situation, either by a new application for such powers under a Light Railway Order, or for the Local Authority to use its compulsory purchase powers. He added that the promoters would do all that could be done to seek a fair price for the trackbed with compensatory arrangements for the parts in commercial use.

Sir Derek explained that witnesses would refer to the County Structure Plan, and the Ministry of Agriculture, Food and Fisheries Report, which showed that the land was poor in agricultural terms and, being designated Type 2 by the County Council, was land where recreational preference should be given. The amount of usable agricultural and forestry land on the trackbed was insignificant in the overall County plan. He also explained that evidence would be given on the financial arrangements of the proposals spread over 15 years. Time was on the promoters side, he said.

The first witness for the railway was Tony Sharp of Messrs Ayling & Strudwick. He gave the planning history from the original approval to extend 860m northwards in 1973, application to extend to West Hoathly which was refused in 1975, and the current application made in 1978, and refused in 1979. He mentioned the recommendations for approval by District and County Planning Officers which was rejected by the council. Next he explained the proposed extension route, the current ownership, and use made of those parts in commercial use. Some two thirds of the trackbed were either overgrown, or in the ownership of British Rail or the Bluebell. Mention was made of Imberhorne Tip, though more detailed evidence was to follow later. He continued, explaining the landscape of the area, difficult access to Horsted Keynes and the direct link with British Rail which should reduce traffic levels at the two existing points of access to the railway.

Mr Wood, Counsel for MSDC, NFU and Hiltons rose to cross examine. For all those giving evidence to the inquiry this was the uncomfortable bit, as each one faced probing, pertinent and challenging questions. Why didn't Bluebell buy the trackbed in 1964? Tony Sharp explained that Bluebell hadn't the resources then, and no-one could really have known how railway preservation was to take off over the following 10 years. Questions on the evidence, the environment and noise levels, followed over some one and a half hours, but Tony remained unshaken throughout the questioning.

Bernard Holden followed, giving a very detailed history of the society from the first meeting, its growth in membership, and the success story of steadily increasing attraction to the present rate in excess of 300,000 passenger journeys each year, the record of preservation of locomotives and rolling stock, the substantial facilities of the workshops, the loco shed, the carriage shed, and also the museums. He also gave details of operation, tourism, educational opportunities and then set out the reasons for and the many advantages the extension would offer, not just advantages for the railway but a means of helping countless thousands to see the railway and the area of outstanding natural beauty, and at the same time reducing traffic levels on the local roads. His detailed analysis covered the future development of the railway, and the alternatives to the Northern Extension. Finally, he gave details of fire precautions, the impressive record since the exceptionally dry year of 1976, and details of trading accounts showing how the railway helped many local firms and thus helped employment and business in the area.

Cross examination began on day two. Having such detailed evidence, Bernard faced long arduous questioning. Asked if the MSDC had not been helpful to the railway, he replied that the officers had been helpful but he had seen some

Some members of the Bluebell team during the public inquiry: (from left) George Nickson, Graham Flight, Peter Thomas, Sir Derek Walker-Smith QC, Eian Caws, Bernard Holden and David Ratcliffe.
GRAHAM FLIGHT

With a blind leap of faith, the railway came to the Public Inquiry at a stage when it only owned one extension plot – the site of West Hoathly station. Here C Class No 31724 stops with a train for East Grinstead. RK BLENCOWE COLLECTION

of the goings-on referred to by Sir Derek in the council meetings and felt the railway had been badly treated. Why do you need five more miles, what is wrong with the present successful operation? Why isn't it enough? Doesn't bus and British Rail currently bring people to the railway? Will people really pay more for a longer ride? Has the railway reached its peak, heading for decline in the future? The questions came thick and fast, and despite the tirade, Bernard remained cool, calm and collected throughout. He seemed to anticipate the hidden reason behind the questions and remained steadfast.

In the re-examination which followed, Councillor Knighton's question to the chairman, asking whether all the councillors still opposed the Bluebell Extension was mentioned and Mr Caws, Junior Counsel for the railway read out the chairman's reply in full, including the passage that the council couldn't change its mind at this late stage or it might have to pay the railway's costs.

Next came Alfred Cantrell, a fellow of the Institute of Civil Engineers, and formerly chief civil engineer, British Railways, Southern Region, who is consultant engineer to the Extension Company. He gave an engineering description of the proposed route, explaining that a minor underbridge had been demolished, but the main earthworks and structures remained largely intact with the tunnel under 'care and maintenance' attention and the viaduct fully maintained as a structure in use. Relaying the track would start from the south, with the tip excavated last.

The railway had engaged the services of agricultural experts – Rural Planning Services. Roger Sayce of that firm, came next, giving his assessment of the effect of relaying the railway on agricultural forestry and horticultural use made of some parts of the trackbed. He suggested substantial accommodation works would be necessary at Hazelden Farm, alternative land

would be required at Birch Farm Nursery, and re-siting of the sheep facilities would be required at Horsted House Farm. He explained difficulties and delays occasioned by the NFU instruction to farmers not to co-operate, though individual farmers had been helpful prior to the Inquiry. Cross-Examination produced a strong exchange to the suggestion had not replied to the NFU. Mr Sayce explained that it took him 18 months to obtain a copy of the MAFF assessment from the District Council.

At this stage a document showing present usage of the trackbed was agreed between Mr Stagg, Principal Planning Officer, and Mike Grant and put to the Inspector. More than 2/3rds was available for purchase or overgrown and unused as at June 1983.

David Morgan chairman of the North Norfolk Railway, vice chairman of the ARPS and chairman of the Transport Trust came to give evidence on behalf of the railway. He explained the railway preservation movement, with many moves nationwide to join up with British Rail by extension projects. He showed how other railways operated and raised finance, such as the Ffestiniog which had just completed its extension and how a 10-12 mile line was about the optimum. Reference was also made to the ARPS and its arbitration service. The link with BR at Sheringham had considerably increased the viability of the BR line.

Financial matters were covered by Graham Flight. This ranged from the cost of the project at £2.25m to the 15 year time scale for construction.

"the council's policies over the matter were bizarre, Gilbertian and bearing the aspects of a Mad Hatter's tea party..."

That period was in three phases, acquisition of trackbed, construction and excavation of the Tip. Graham went into detail about funding options from public issues of shares to charitable subscriptions. He completed his evidence with steps agreed by the directors should the Inquiry confirm the refusal of Planning Permission by the sale of West Hoathly station site to defray the costs of the Inquiry.

There followed the usual cross examination and the Inspector asked about the basis of 2/3rds of the membership paying £1 per week for 10 years being sufficient to fund the project.

David Ratcliff, chairman of the Extension Company followed, giving the history of the Extension proposals, the relationship with Bluebell Railway Ltd and the Society. He explained how responsible the railway was, hence its cautious approach to the extension, not really actively pursued until a sound base had been established. He explained the reasons the railway had not incorporated a request for compulsory purchase powers and the emphasis on acquisition by negotiation. He also explained how the railway would be built, and that the Bluebell Railway would operate trains and either maintain the extension, or provide the money for the Extension Company to do so.

David, as expected, faced a barrage of questions, particularly about the acquisition of land and the issue of compulsory purchase. He showed that land does change hands on average every seven years in the area. He also explained that negotiations to date led him to a different

conclusion, in reply to a direct question (or statement), the owners would not sell. Despite concerted questioning, he emerged relatively unscathed.

Mr Brian Scott Divisional Manager, British Rail Southern Region, Central Division, gave evidence in support. The extension of the Bluebell was likely to increase the passenger flow on the East Grinstead service by 10% at off-peak times. Decisions on long-term finance such as stock renewal and electrification would be affected by the outcome of the Inquiry. He repeated that British Rail saw the extension as a social benefit.

For the South East Tourist Board, Mr Fred Cubbage gave evidence that the board supported the Bluebell. He explained that the railway was one of the top tourist attractions in the area, and coupled with the Sheffield Park House and the National Trust Gardens added considerably to the tourist attractions. A connection with British Rail and the Worth Way gave enhanced leisure opportunities.

Mr Allen Pull on behalf of East Grinstead Chamber of Commerce supported the extension proposals, and Mr Hartland representing the East Grinstead Society gave a reasoned case of support. He referred to the new town and district consultative document and said the railway fitted in to the overall concept, would help keep the national railway network and offer leisure and training opportunities for those living nearby. He was cross-examined at length while his evidence was probed and tested.

Next to follow was Ron Potter, our planning expert. In terms of evidence you could say this was the big one, lasting for a day and a half. Ron is a senior planning officer with the London Borough of Hillingdon and has been involved in the Maplin proposals and movement of waste by rail. The planning aspects were thoroughly examined, and Ron explained how the railway provided a valuable informal recreation facility, not only for working members but also for 200,000 visitors annually. He produced analysis of accident statistics in Sussex and of fire and safety records nationwide, with reference to preserved railways. The extension would help reduce traffic in the vicinity of Horsted Keynes, while evidence was given about the growth of leisure activities and likely changes in the area with the completion of the M25. He showed how the extension conformed with county council policies and would benefit East Grinstead commercially. Reference was made to the East Grinstead and Worth District plan which had been issued for consultative purposes.

The railway has raised objections as it is not mentioned in the leisure activities in the area.

Ron continued with the visitor survey taken on Vintage Sunday, the house to house survey at Sharpthorne and the 633 replies to the leaflet distribution in East Grinstead. A review of the catchment area in relation to the K&ESR and Mid-Hants Railways was also given, together with a detailed appraisal and comparison with other preserved railways. Agricultural considerations were covered, purporting to show that the refusal of planning permission was unsound. Trespass and noise was also covered in detail and despite a lack of response from the council as to noise evidence beforehand, some measure of agreement was achieved at the Inquiry.

Very detailed evidence was given about the

Tip, its formation, an adverse report from the Ombudsman, the full level of statutory controls, probable sites to deposit the rubbish and the likely cost, together with a letter from the research establishment at Harwell which showed some interest in examination and monitoring the excavation.

With so much information, and such painstaking thorough coverage of each facet, it was inevitable that the cross-examination would be long. Ron answered every question in so much depth that it was difficult to keep track of detail.

Alan Brodrick was called to give evidence as to the costing of re-laying the railway in the light of evidence to come from Mr Hilton. He explained how he had arrived at his figures taking each section one by one to arrive at the overall figure, by normal estimating methods.

Now we turn to the objectors. For convenience, Mr Harding of Keepers Cottage, Kingscote came first. He explained how he used the trackbed for a duck breeding pond and to cross his four ewes over to a grazing patch on the other side of the trackbed. He explained how he had searched far and wide for a suitable property and found Keepers in 1978. In answer to Sir Derek, in cross-examination he agreed he had taken a chance that the East Grinstead bypass and

gas main would not use the trackbed and the Bluebell Extension would not come to fruition.

For Council Bill Hatton was the sole witness. In the event the chairman, Colonel Major did not give evidence nor did Harry Sharp the Environmental Officer, despite what was reported in the local paper. The evidence covered the history of the planning and Light Railway Order applications. Reference was made to representations made to the council and with specific reference to the Tip, he said he was not happy that the tip could be moved in 15 years time. He gave detailed comments on the proposals, stressing that the council was not opposing the existing Bluebell Railway, which was thought of as a valued recreational facility. Comments on area plans were next made with particular reference to the area being designated one of outstanding natural beauty, and the county tourist policy. Other matters raised were noise levels, traffic levels and increased activity if the proposal was allowed. Details of the trackbed as existing were given followed by the council's reasons for refusal of planning permission. Precise use of the track bed for agricultural purposes was also given in the detailed evidence. As to the Light Railway Order application, the council felt it was a matter for the Secretary of State and his professional advisers.

The northern end of the proposed extension, the town of East Grinstead and the 10-arch Imberhorne Viaduct to the south.
PHILIP LANE PHOTOGRAPHY

purchased in 1981, and the effect of the railway extension on the farm. The information showed the railway had not affected the value in 1981. Mr Hilton explained he had not offered Mr Sayce the opportunity to view the farm, as Mr Sayce had arrived unannounced one Saturday thus offering no chance to consult the NFU beforehand. Mr Hilton accepted that he was trespassing when he took some of the photographs which he offered in evidence.

Mr John Robson of Northwood Farm in partnership with Mr Hilton gave evidence next. He explained clearly and concisely the sheep farming methods in use on the trackbed and their success so far. In cross-examination he explained the only suitable alternatives for the sheep operation, and the need for good access from one part of the farm to another.

The tenant at Hill Place Farm, situated between the viaduct and the tip Mr Leonard Hobbs spoke of his opposition. He did not use the trackbed but feared the excavation of the tip, having suffered considerably from flies and pests during the tipping years ago.

Mr Christopher May of Hazelden Farm, just south of the tip came next. Mr May operated a sizeable dairy farm of 154 cows on some 310 acres. He described his farming methods and the use made of the trackbed for access, and winter feeding. The inspector was informed that major accommodation works had been suggested by Mr Sayce either a new bridge or resiting of the farm buildings north of the trackbed. The railway acknowledged that some major alternative would be necessary. Mr May was also concerned about noise effect on his milk yield, the fire risk and explained that the tip removal might affect the bacteria count upon which his milk was priced. Mr May also expressed concern that the alternative proposals did not go far enough to redress the effect on the farm.

At Birch Farm Nursery, Mr Ingwersen with his brother had established an internationally recognised business of collecting and propagating alpine plants and used part of the former trackbed for standing out the plants. The inspector was informed that the railway proposed to offer alternative adjacent land for this purpose, though at this stage no specific proposals had been put. M. Ingwersen explained the nursery methods; its 50 year establishment and its success in its specialist field. At any one time some 70,000 plants could be standing on the former trackbed. He also expressed the dangers of fire from the railway, particularly in periods of dry weather.

Mr Alec Leggat who farms at Mill Place Farm, Kingscote, explained his farming operations with 82 cows and 75 followers. He used the trackbed as a source of timber for the farm, and for a water pipe. He expressed concern about the effect of the passage of trains on his animals, and the disruption caused during construction. He endorsed fears of fires and objected to proximity of the proposed railway on nearby property. He also felt strongly that the railway should have purchased the track from BR when it came up for sale.

The last farmer to give evidence was Mr John Foster of Ash Lea Farm, Kingscote. He explained

There next followed the cross examination by Sir Derek. Like the railway witnesses, Bill Hatton faced considerable questioning which lasted over a day. He was asked in what capacity he gave evidence for the council, and who was to give evidence on Council policy. He was asked how he could say professionally he was opposed when his predecessor, the WSCC Planning Officer, ESCC, Wealden District Council and the railway's Planning Officer all professionally supported the project. The various structure plans were examined, as were references to noise, traffic and disturbance aspects unsupported by any analysis. Sir Derek suggested the Council was in league with the NFU, quoting from the local press statements made by councillors. The case for the council was then completed and the Inquiry went on to consider the case for Hilton Investments Ltd.

Mr Ian Hilton of Horsted House Farm gave evidence against the extension. His objections came into three categories – amenity, agriculture and effect on the surrounding area – he explained that his property in an area of outstanding natural beauty enjoyed splendid views. The present railway activity of whistles and station announcements already intruded on his amenities and any extension would bring the railway within 100 yards of his house and adjacent to a nearby cottage. People visiting the railway trespassed and picnicked on his land. In agricultural terms he showed how he used the former trackbed for sheep handling, winter feeding and access to the lower part of the farm. The passage of steam engines would also endanger his farm by fire risk. Already the railway brought people to the surrounding area, and the long 15 year construction period, coupled with more visitors would have a detrimental effect on the surrounding area. Mr Hilton questioned the costing of the extension and said his estimators had come up with a construction figure of £2.7m without land acquisition. He also felt Bluebell was not capable of achieving the extension, and showed photographs of existing fencing and hedges along the present line, and also of the tunnel at Sharpthorne.

In cross-examination, Mr Hilton agreed his main occupation was that of a Property Developer and that if farming offered tax concessions he would probably take advantage of them. He was questioned about his costings, and the methods used which he agreed was the cost of constructing yards of trackbed and drainage and multiplying by 11,000. In answer to Sir Derek, he agreed he personally had no qualifications as a builder. Some information was given about the value of the farm, having been he used his half of the trackbed and rented other parts of access for his cows to rented grazing fields. He also took silage from other fields which would necessitate crossing the trackbed frequently (up to 80 times) on three days each year. Mr Foster explained how the railway on an embankment would affect his peace and quiet on a Sunday, and could necessitate felling a number of trees around the vicinity of farm crossing to enable adequate visibility.

Mr Shaun Leavey, secretary of the local National Farmers Union gave evidence opposing the extension. He gave the history of the opposition, and felt the proposals were against the national agricultural interest. The farmers objected in principle having bought the trackbed 20 years ago in good faith, he said; the NFU supported them. He made reference to individual farms, supporting the objectors on problems such as fire risk, pest control, weed control, and stockproof fencing. Lastly he mentioned the question of crossings and how dangerous these were to slow moving farm machinery, and concluded that the NFU was adamantly opposed to the proposals.

> **"The farmers objected in principle having bought the trackbed 20 years ago in good faith, he said; the NFU supported them."**

Detailed and lengthy cross-examination followed as each and every statement was questioned. Was the degree of use of the trackbed put to the NFU meeting? Was the issue really discussed? Two landowners had given evidence they are farming at a loss – the land is low quality, the Weald has special problems due to clay – how can it really affect the National Farming Interest. Was the NFU dictum of non co-operation unhelpful to the Inspector? Mr Leavey

said the inspector should be made aware of the strength of feeling among his members. He quoted a letter from Bill Brophy in the East Grinstead Courier in 1979 which said Bluebell would not go for Compulsory Purchase powers, but Sir Derek stated that the true position was that if a landowner held the scheme to ransom the railway might have to review the position. This had been made known to the local MP in a letter written in 1978 by Nick Stanbury on behalf of the Extension Company as a statement of policy.

On and on went the questioning about fires, needs, fencing difficulties with BR, and difficulties with the Bluebell.

Three people came forward to speak:

Mrs Linsall of Northwood House, handed in a petition from local residents, taken just prior to the Inquiry, of persons opposed to the extension proposals.

Mr Wykeham-Martin read his prepared evidence. He referred to his earlier objections made to the Secretary of State in 1978, and that he now lived on a different farm with two fields adjoining the Sharpthorne Road at Horsted. On busy days cars parked all over the place. He quoted statistics from *Bluebell News* about cars parked at the railway, and reiterated his opposition to the proposals. He was not cross-examined by either Counsel.

Mr James Stuchlik of West Chiltington spoke for the general public. He was not a member of the society, and didn't know the extension people until he came to the inquiry on the last two days. He spoke as a father and grandfather of the leisure and pleasure given to thousands and thousands who visit the Bluebell. The railway was there for 80 years and farming went on without difficulty – could it not do so again? The extension was like a surgeon replacing a severed arm which would benefit the public.

There followed the final submissions by Counsel. Mr Wood for the objectors said, it had been a remarkable inquiry, being the first occasion a disused railway line had been fragmented by so many uses. He said the Bluebell men were not arrogant men, yet there was a perception in their minds that made their proposals arrogant. The extension was, he said, not essential to the Bluebell Railway and its objectives. Sir Derek made the final submissions, picking out the issues as stated by the Inspector at the pre-inquiry meeting and showing the evidence given in relation to those issues. He mentioned that farming was a secondary interest to two objectors, to provide benefits for tax losses, and that agriculture was not a sacred cow, The whole proposal was not for profit but for public benefit. This issue will be decided by which side provides the greatest public benefit, he said.

With the inquiry at an end, over the next two days the Inspector visited Sheffield Park and Horsted Keynes, travelled behind Blackmoor Vale in the Observation Coach and inspected bridges, fences, and noted noise levels. Accompanied by Bill Hatton representing the Council and Peter Thomas representing the Bluebell he walked the entire route of the extension, visited farms along the way, and the proximity of houses to the railway mentioned in letters.

The inspector will now sift through the evidence and make his recommendations to the Secretary of State for the Environment, in respect of the planning appeal and to the Secretary of State for Transport in respect of the application for a Light Railway Order. It is likely to be some time before the respective Ministers' views are known.

It was to be another year (the end of 1984) before the railway would buy its next plot of land, Kingscote station, seen here slumbering at the point of purchase by Bluebell. **BOB BAMBEROUGH**

Recommendations

by Mike Grant

The Inspecting Officer's report was made in a letter to The Secretary of State for the Environment dated 2 April 1985 nearly two years after the inquiry had taken place. It is a very detailed letter (70 pages long which is far too long to detail) but he made the following comments and recommendations:

Report by The Inspecting Officer for the Department of the Environment

Comment

While the planning history of the project made it reasonable to entertain the hope that planning permission would be granted on appeal, the proposal itself could not be carried out without the acquisition of land. The basis for a rational assessment of the poor prospects of acquisition has been available for a significant period: it seems to me that the promoters, in pursuing the order application, have behaved unreasonably.

Recommendations

I recommend that the application for the Bluebell Light Railway Order 1982 be refused.

I recommend that the appeal under Section 36 of the Town and Country Planning Act be dismissed.

Accordingly, I recommend that costs should not be awarded in relation to the planning appeal, but if powers are available to the Secretary of State for Transport, such an award in relation to the Light Railway Order would be appropriate.

It seems to me that the Inspecting Officer may not have had sufficient information regarding developments and negotiations with landowners since the inquiry closed. Horsted House Farm had changed hands again and the new owner was much more friendly and co-operative. Development on other negotiations had taken place but it is reasonable to understand that land acquisition would be unwise if the project could not go forward. It also appears to me that the Inspector left a door open for the Secretary of State for Transport to overrule and approve the LRO which would in turn enable the planning appeal to be made.

In a letter also dated 2 April 1985 from the Department of Transport the Inspector said:

Departments of the Environment and Transport
South East Regional Office
Charles House 375 Kensington High Street London W14 8QH
Telephone 01-603 3444 ext

tt

Messrs Adam Burn & Metson
4 Staple Inn
Holborn
LONDON
WC1V 7QW

Your reference
MGC/KFB
Our reference
APP/5405/A/80/00151
Date
− 2 APR 1985

Gentlemen

TOWN AND COUNTRY PLANNING ACT 1971 − SECTION 36
APPEAL BY BLUEBELL EXTENSION RAILWAY LIMITED
APPLICATION No. HO/39/78

1. I am directed by the Secretary of State for the Environment to say that consideration has been given to the report of the Inspector Mr Stephen Marks MA RIBA who held a local inquiry into your clients' appeal against the decision of Mid Sussex District Council to refuse planning permission for the construction of a railway between Horsted Keynes Station and East Grinstead Station, West Sussex. Also considered at the local inquiry was an application to the Secretary of State for Transport made by your clients for an order entitled the Bluebell Extension Light Railway Order.

2. The Department's letter of 22 March 1983 indicated that on the basis that the application for planning permission, which is the subject of this appeal, was made by a Statutory Undertaker to develop operational land, the appeal would be determined jointly by the Secretaries of State for the Environment and Transport in accordance with Section 225 of the 1971 Act. However, in a letter of 29 March 1984, the Department explained that it had subsequently been advised that although the Bluebell Railway Ltd is a Statutory Undertaker, the Bluebell Extension Railway Ltd is not, and that as the planning appeal does not therefore involve operational land it falls to be determined by the Secretary of State for the Environment alone. The letter also confirmed that the application for a Light Railway Order is a matter for the Department of Transport alone. Accordingly this letter is concerned only with the consideration of the planning appeal and its purpose is to convey the decision of the Secretary of State for the Environment in respect of that appeal. A further letter will be issued in due course about the application for costs made at the inquiry in connection with the planning appeal.

3. A copy of the Inspector's report is enclosed and his full conclusions are contained in Annex A to this letter. The Inspector recommended that the planning appeal be dismissed.

4. The Inspector's conclusions on the planning appeal have been carefully considered as have all the arguments advanced for and against your clients' proposal. It is noted that the existing Bluebell Line which has been operating in East and West Sussex since 1960, is considered by the South of England Tourist Board

1

The Inspecting Officer's weighty report document, which came two years after the Public Inquiry, in April 1985.

The Secretary of State has carefully considered the Inspector's recommendation. He has concluded, however, that your clients did not act unreasonably in submitting an application for a Light Railway Order, which he has now decided to make. In the circumstances the Secretary of State does not consider it appropriate to make an award for costs.

In the end this did open the way for the planning application to be approved. It is interesting to note that The County Planning Officer, in his report dated 3 August 1979

said that:

"The County Council, having regard to the policies for recreation and the countryside in the submitted structure plan, has given its support to the proposal. The support is based upon the conclusion of the County Council's Coast and Countryside Committee that there are clear recreational advantages which outweigh the detriment to farming interests. Bearing in mind the advice given by the Ministry of Agriculture, and the points made in other representations and the support given by the County Council, I have

come to the view that the balance of evidence would indicate that the application should be recommended for approval."

This was to be subject to conditions which were followed when the LRO was applied for, such as phasing, fencing, fire control, clearance of vegetation, removal of waste from Imberhorne Cutting etc. It is difficult to understand why the District Council and the Inspector at the Inquiry did not follow this recommendation as it would have saved so much time and expense to all involved.

When Bluebell demolished its own extension!

by Klaus Marx

The contract for lifting the remaining disused line west and north of Horsted Keynes by British Railways in 1964 was awarded to the Demolition and Construction Co of Croydon, which had just previously completed the lifting of the Hawkhurst branch and the line to Newhaven West Quay.

The contract was contained under two schedules.

The first concerned the lifting of the track from Ardingly to just short of the crossover – a few dozen yards from Horsted Keynes signalbox – and to restart at milepost 11 at the Leamland overbridge (north of Horsted Keynes station) to the south end of Hill Place Viaduct (Imberhorne).

The second schedule concerned the demolition of specified bridges and structures. The brick underbridge at Coombe (just north of West Hoathly) to be demolished to 3ft above road level. Only one other bridge was to receive the contractor's attention, that immediately south of Kingscote station where only the brick parapet was to be taken down to rail level and concrete weathering capping to be laid on top of the exposed brickwork.

The signalbox at Kingscote was to be taken down, as at West Hoathly where the station's footbridge was also blacklisted. The contractor quite sensibly started at Ardingly and worked northwards with temporary bases at West Hoathly and later Kingscote. Lifting at Ardingly started on 15 July.

Along with various wagons, the contractor also brought a four-wheel Ruston & Hornsby diesel No 269 595 of 1949. It failed on the start day, getting out of control between Horsted Keynes and West Hoathly, the driver having tried to stop it by engaging reverse gear with disastrous results internally. This lay in the down Lewes platform at Horsted Keynes for several days, but by early August was back at West Hoathly.

The same day it had met with disaster was the first of working with a steam locomotive hired from the Bluebell, producing both the adhesive and braking power needed for the 1 in 75 grades which predominate on this northern section.

The Bluebell's North London Railway tank locomotive No 2650 was on for the first three weeks, replaced by No 473 *Birch Grove* for a few days following 6 August to enable No 2650 to have a boiler wash-out.

The latter was on duty again until 30 August and No 473 then filled in a few more days in early September.

The turn leaves Sheffield Park soon after 7am and usually returns coupled to the rear locomotive of the 5.25pm from Horsted Keynes, with the Bluebell's Fred Cleaver and Jack Owen on footplate duty.

An item that survived the demolition at West Hoathly is the former postbox that was set in the wall of the building on the forecourt side.
COLIN TYSON

The scene looking north at West Hoathly in October 1964, with the Bluebell's North London Railway loco No 2650 on track-lifting duties. The footbridge was first to be demolished because one of the cranes was delivered to Ardingly by mistake and therefore the crews at West Hoathly needed 'something to be getting on with'.
SR CLARK

The strategic outpost

The editorial column in *Bluebell News* Autumn 1975 made mention of a notice inserted in the previous issue (Summer 1975) regarding the immediate need for funds which have to be raised if there was a possibility of an extension northwards from Horsted Keynes.

The editorial read: "Members will know that the West Hoathly site is a key one, because if this becomes a residential development the way to East Grinstead is blocked for ever.

"It is fair to report that there is a conflict of views among the working members about the merits of the extension proposals. Some feel that we have enough track and active rolling stock to maintain; at the other end of the spectrum there are other members who feel that East Grinstead with its connection with British Rail must be our goal. In between are others who see a compromise of making West Hoathly as a reasonable target for which to aim.

A not inconsiderable number of members have drawn attention to the dangers of stagnation and of not looking for ways of expansion to attract visitors again and again. It was with these views in mind that your committee agreed to an investigation of the possibility of re-opening to East Grinstead. Had they not taken this approach they could have been accused of being complacent or unimaginative.

The need to secure West Hoathly site now presents a good opportunity for the membership and other supporters of the railway to show their feelings about the extension.

Waiting for trains again: Sharpthorne Tunnel south portal in February 1990. MIKE ESAU

Messrs Ayling & Strudwick
Land surveyors and valuers
Burgess Hill

27 March 1975

Re: Site of West Hoathly Railway Station

Dear Mr Holden
At your request, I have examined the plan submitted by M.P. Harris (Holdings) Ltd to develop this site, which is understood to be owned by them.

The site extends to about 1.5 acres, and the Application Plan provides for Hamsey Road and Station Road to be linked. To the frontage of Station Road it is proposed that a Terrace of 6 houses and a Semi-detached pair be erected, with a block of garages at the rear of the Terrace; while fronting the proposed Link Road, 5 pairs of Semi-detached Houses are shown, having garages adjacent to these. A total of 18 houses and garages.

In my opinion, the value of the whole site is between £24,000 and £30,000. There seems to be the possibility that the prospective developers purchased the site for as much as £70,000. This, two or three years ago, would not have been unreasonable, and if the Bluebell Extension Company were to ask to purchase the whole of the site, they may well be asked for this figure, as the developers might claim that by selling they were also losing their building profit and, therefore, the opportunity of at least recovering their losses.

Having examined the proposed layout plan, it does seem possible that a railway could still be laid through the Site, and for it to remain possible to build about 10 houses. The value of the Site of the 8 houses would be some £16,000 to £20,000, but it might also be claimed that the value of the remaining sites would be depreciated by the construction of the railway.

As far as I can see at the moment, I would be very loathed to advise the Extension Company to purchase the whole site with a view to selling off sites for 10 or more houses, bearing in mind the depressed market.

Remember, if you are in favour of the extension proposals being pursued then your support is necessary now. Once houses are built where K Class moguls passed on the 3.28pm Haywards Heath to London Bridge, or a C2X shunted the goods, it is too late.

If you are a member who wishes to see your railway reach out beyond the confines of the present line please make whatever contribution you can towards the current appeal fund as soon as possible."

Meanwhile, earlier in the year, Bluebell and extension committee member Bernard Holden had received this piece of 'advice' from Bluebell's land agents, shown left.

Bluebell News Winter 1975 reported in one line:
STOP PRESS. West Hoathly site secured. Full details next issue.

The same issue also reported an early flurry of specific extension fundraising in the shape of Alf and Kathy Castle, who have a fruit and vegetable stall at Sheffield Park station, running various raffles and competitions for 'extension funds'.

An enclosed and secured civil engineers' depot was established on the railway's land at West Hoathly prior to the arrival of track, allowing attention to be afforded to matters such as the drainage of the site. MIKE ESAU

Planning permission granted to develo

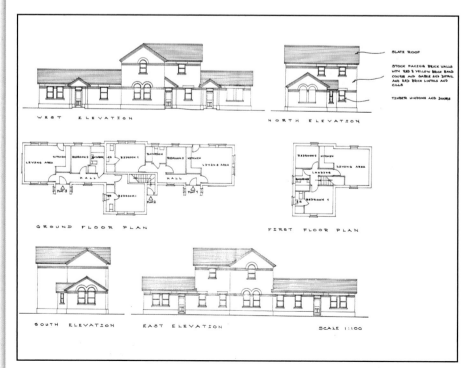

SLATE ROOF

STOCK FACING BRICK WALLS WITH RED & YELLOW BRICK BAND COURSE AND GABLE END DETAIL AND RED BRICK LINTOLS AND CILLS

TIMBER WINDOWS AND DOORS

WEST ELEVATION

NORTH ELEVATION

LIVING AREA   KITCHEN   BEDROOM 1   BATHROOM   BEDROOM 1   BATHROOM   BEDROOM 2   KITCHEN   LIVING AREA

HALL   HALL

FLAT 3   BEDROOM 1   FLAT 1

GROUND FLOOR PLAN

BEDROOM 2   KITCHEN

LANDING   LIVING AREA

BEDROOM 1

FIRST FLOOR PLAN

SOUTH ELEVATION   EAST ELEVATION   SCALE 1:100

Mid Sussex District Council has given permission for Bluebell Railway plc to constru a station house and a pair of three-bedroome semi-detached cottages at the site of West Hoathly station, Sharpthorne, West Sussex.

The station house would contain three two-bedroomed flats.

The Bluebell application included the statement: "The intention of the proposal is to re-create an ensemble of railway style buildings to include the reconstruction of t former station building, much in its origina position, and the development of a pair of railway style semi-detached cottages at the end of Hamsey Road.

The proposed development does not prejudice the safeguarding of sufficient lanc within West Hoathly Goods Yard for a stati halt to be erected should this be a feasible proposition at a later date.

The reconstructed station building will b sub-divided into three two-bedroom apartments with communal gardens and ca parking area. The semi-detached cottages w face the railway and each comprises three bedrooms with private gardens and

Looking north at West Hoathly in February 1991 and the bridge sections for what will become the new bridge for New Coombe lay in waiting. MIKE ESAU

West Hoathly station area

Published in *Bluebell News* Summer 2009

mmunal parking area with a single access
int on Hamsey Road."

"The station house and the railway cottages
ll be constructed of local stock facing
icks with red and yellow band course and
ble end detail and red brick lintels and cills
th slate roof – similar in design to the
lage stations on railway lines to the north
d east of East Grinstead – for instance at
ormans, Lingfield, Hever, Cowden and
ithyham. The fenestration and detailing
ll be of painted woodwork to match
isting station houses of the period."

A total of 16 letters of objection to the
velopment were considered by the
anning committees, and there was one
tter of support for the proposals.

It is thought that the development would
nerate around a fifth of the total still to
ise towards delivering the railway to
ast Grinstead.

The provision of adding a platform for
assenger use at West Hoathly would be
e subject of separate planning consent, to
considered at an appropriate time in
e future.

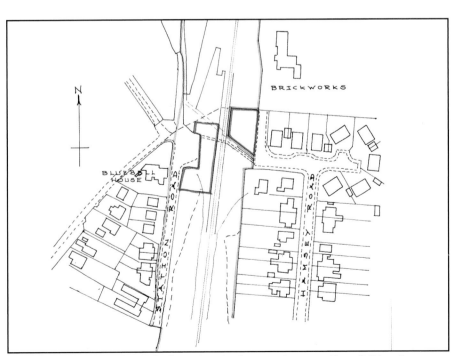

West Hoathly location plan with planned station house and cottages (in red). WEALD DESIGNS

Physical progress:
First track panel laid

by Michael Welch

On 13 March 1988, the Bluebell Railway ceremonially laid the first section of track on its extension from Horsted Keynes to East Grinstead, laid by the Rt Hon Paul Channon MP, Secretary of State for Transport.

Sunday 13 March 1988 dawned grey and uninviting but the V.I.P train waiting at Sheffield Park looked immaculate and the principal dining carriages of TO No 1309 and RMB No 1818 had tables meticulously laid. The 11.42 train took guests including Ian Allan, Michael Harris and Handel Kardas from *Railway World* and Chris Green, director Network SouthEast. Roger Price was train manager and newly appointed catering manager Mike Sharland was on duty for the first time with Sandra Noel as head waitress and Samantha Brewer and Rupert Bungard chefs for the day.

Guest of Honour, The Rt Hon Paul Channon MP, Secretary of state for Transport, arrived and was introduced to the chairmen of the boards (plc, operating and extension) and their wives by the Hon Ralph Montagu, representing Lord Montagu, president of Bluebell Railway plc.

On arrival at Horsted Keynes the GNR directors saloon and LNWR observation car were hauled up to Leamland Bridge by North London Railway loco No 58850 – how appropriate that it was this loco, which had been used on track lifting operations north of Horsted Keynes in the 1960s, was now participating in the relaying of the permanent way it had helped to remove 25 years ago!

The tracklaying task had been rehearsed repeatedly prior to the event and the steam crane performed faultlessly as Mr Channon, now wearing a hard hat, operated the various levers with great dexterity under the watchful eye of Neil Cameron, the crane supervisor. All too soon it was over and all that remained was to secure screws in the sleeper chairs. Mr Channon then proceeded to the stand for the speeches to commence. Bernard Holden spoke first and welcomed Mr Channon, his wife and other guests. Mr Channon spoke of his great pleasure to be present and praised the volunteers. He stressed the great success of the railway as one of the nation's leading steam railways. His remarks brought warm applause from spectators and the crane tooted in appreciation.

The chairman of Mid Sussex District Council, Christopher Snowling, endorsed the Secretary of State's remarks and wished the Bluebell success as it moved northwards.

BRPS chairman Terry Cole spoke of the significance of the date. The original preservation society had been formed 29 years ago that week.

At this point it was arranged that the Bluebell's Michael Hawkins and Felix Cope, representing the youngest and oldest volunteers respectively, would complete the task by tightening the fishplate bolts.

Terry Cole, speaking to a Radio Sussex

A modest chalked notice at Horsted Keynes says it all as it makes reference to East Grinsted (sic).

reporter, refused to be drawn on the question of a completion date for the extension scheme. However, he anticipated a 10-12 year timescale.

After an excellent meal the special train returned to Sheffield Park at 2.25pm and so ended one of the most momentous days in Bluebell history. Even the rain didn't let things down, which started around 5pm, by which time most guests and visitors were on their way home.

The steam crane gang: back row (from left) Geoff Stringer, Trevor West, (Hon Paul Channon), Neil Cameron and Brian Hopkins. Front row (from left) Andy Wilkins, Louise Bellingham and Paul Russell.

Neil Cameron (below) and Paul Channon enter the scene.

The track section is nearly in place.

Paul Channon poses for the camera after his official duty.

In at the start: Distinguished guests and visitors assemble at Leamland Bridge, just north of Horsted Keynes, for the ceremonial laying of the first track panel on the northern extension, 13 March 1988. **ALL: MIKE ESAU**

Phase 1
Horsted Keynes to Horsted Keynes Farm

In the autumn of 1987, the breakthrough came that allowed plans to be made to physically start the extension project – the acquisition of the trackbed immediately north of Horsted Keynes. It was certainly an exciting time for Bluebell members, who had just witnessed the electrification of the BR line to East Grinstead with the official start of the new electric service on 30 September, 1987. On 19 September, Class 73 locomotive No 73004 had been named *The Bluebell Railway* in a ceremony at East Grinstead. With all the optimism in the world, it really seemed that we would be at East Grinstead ourselves in no time at all.

In early 1988, the directors of the Extension Company invited civil engineer Steve Johnstone to join the Board and duly appointed him project manager for the extension, Steve having been responsible for the dismantling of the former Lingfield station footbridge and its re-erection at Sheffield Park.

By summer 1998 work on the extension had started in earnest and trees and undergrowth were being cleared to allow the fencing gang access to repair or replace the lineside fencing.

Tea-making and messing facilities for extension volunteers were provided by means of a PMV parcels van stabled just north of Leamland Bridge. Track materials for Phase 1 were estimated at £64,800 with £8,100 needed to be raised for buying rail by the end of October 1988.

Chaired sleepers laid to the bridge on 6 May, 1989. MIKE ESAU

From Leamland Bridge the brave new extension stretches north to Horsted House Farm, prior to ballast packing. Permanent Way costs amounted to 70% of the overall Phase 1 budget. MIKE ESAU

North London Railway No 2650 (as British Railways No 58850) conveys volunteers and ballast hoppers to site on Phase 1 on 6 May, 1989. MIKE ESAU

Seen in May 1988, the PMV parcels van for messing facilities just north of Leamland Bridge – the track down from the car park field being ideal for transferring construction materials. MIKE ESAU

An open barn obstructed the right of way at Horsted House Farm, seen in May 1988. Beyond the barn were animal pens and a half-bricked up bridge. MIKE ESAU

Far Left: By the Spring of 1989 trackwork was down and ballasting is under way. Note the use of the North London Railway tank loco, perhaps redeeming itself for having lifted this section of track in 1964. MIKE ESAU

Left: Horsted House Bridge, May 1989. One half had been bricked up where it was used as a rifle range. The stone bridges on the section north of Horsted Keynes were felt to be more visually attractive than their red-brick counterparts, south of Horsted Keynes. MIKE ESAU

Animal pens just south of Horsted House Bridge on 4 September, 1988, looking south towards Horsted Keynes. MIKE ESAU

Another load of ballast delivered by the ex-London Transport wagon on 20 May, 1989. MIKE ESAU

Do the extension shuttle!

The Department of Transport requirement that the extension should be separated from the rest of the railway and covered by catch point protection was to entail certain revisions of and repairs to the existing layout at Horsted Keynes. Anticipated work in the Autumn of 1989 included relaying the track in No 2 platform followed by necessary signalling alterations.

A full DOT inspection would then be arranged with the intention of opening the extension for public use by Easter 1990 as part of the railway's 30th anniversary celebrations.

Of course it was felt that an 'extension shuttle' service north of Horsted Keynes would both maintain visitor interest and the fact that the railway needed to maximise its new asset in order to recoup some of the £85,000 expended on Phase 1 construction. A 'shuttle and diesel working party' had been set up to consider various options. If passengers were going to travel in reasonable numbers they would have to be encouraged

to purchase a 'package' including a ride on the shuttle upon arrival at Sheffield Park. Properly publicised and marketed, it was felt that 40% of passengers would take the shuttle when it was operating. Traffic figures from March to December for 1988 and 1989 were analysed to see which were the busiest days – shuttle passengers would be expected to leave one train at Horsted Keynes and catch the next train (rather than the same train) back to Sheffield Park.

Subsequently SR Maunsell BCK carriage No 6575, built at Eastleigh in 1929, received modifications to its brake end for use on the shuttle and was turned so that it faced north. SR Open Third No 1309 joined it to make a two-coach train.

Across the north end of No 6575, John Reynard fixed a yellow painted panel into which was let a window and furnished with a windscreen wiper – to facilitate propelling in one direction. On the outside of the panel is a horn worked from a compressor and inside the brake compartment is a console on which is fitted a wiper switch, a button to sound the horn and another which links via a cable fitted along the coaches below body level, to a bell unit carried in the cab of the engine. Two rings on the bell are exchanged between driver and guard to effect a start.

Following an inspection of the whole 10-minute operation of the shuttle by Major Olver on 1 April 1990 he confirmed its operation for public use on 13 April.

With engine whistling forbidden, save in an emergency, the shuttle was under way to the public commencing 14 April. Traffic was an immediate success, 7795 passengers having travelled on the shuttle over the 12 operational days of April, bringing in a revenue of £7114.

On alighting at Horsted Keynes from Sheffield Park, passengers for the Northern Extension Shuttle' (departing from what was Platform 1 at this point in history) would emerge from the subway and pass under this makeshift arch in order to control shuttle ticket inspection and sales. MIKE ESAU

Below: The first shuttle train on opening day arrives at the buffer stops at Horsted House Farm. The bridge still being half-bricked up at this point. MIKE ESAU

Preparations in the sidings on the shuttle train prior to entering platform 1 to pick up passengers. MIKE ESAU

A fully loaded shuttle train on the first day of operation – 14 April 1990. P Class No 323 *Bluebell* propels the two coaches. The brake end modification to carriage No 6575 is clear in this view. MIKE ESAU

Horsted House Farm to Sharpthorne Tunnel

Looking south at Bluebell's limit of operation at Horsted House Farm in November 1990. MIKE ESAU

Tracklaying pushed north again in 1991-1992. SR Q Class No 541 heads north with an engineers' train to the railhead in January 1992 from the viewpoint of Horsted House Farm Bridge. MIKE ESAU

Trackbed cleared and marked out, looking toward the south portal of Sharpthorne Tunnel in the winter of 1991. MICK BLACKBURN

Raising the trackbed formation south of the tunnel. MICK BLACKBURN

Ballasting and tracklaying on the last curve before the south end of the tunnel on 5 February 1992. MIKE ESAU

Sharpthorne Tunnel

The first set of works in the construction of the Lewes & East Grinstead Railway started at West Hoathly and the tunnel under Sharpthorne – it being quite usual for Victorian contractors to make a start with tunnel construction in order that vast amounts of spoil required to embank and fill in other works could be obtained, obviating the need to seek materials from outside the railway.

The tunnel was constructed under the Sharpthorne Ridge and is 731 yards in length. 600 men were employed in its construction and, while built to last, their construction was always fraught with danger; on the morning of 11 October 1879, some brickwork gave way and fell on a navvy, dislocating his shoulder and breaking one of his legs. On 1 December that year Henry Mughal, a native of the village, had a wooden centre supporting a brick arch give way and crushed the victim so that 'he was expired before he could be got out of the tunnel'. Mr William Elliot broke his arm while ascending a tunnel shaft in a basket and colliding against the brickwork.

The final siting of the tunnel was slightly west of what had been originally intended, having been marginally deviated by engineer Wolfe Barry in deference to the opposition of local landowners who maintained its presence would interfere with their hunting and game shooting.

The final choice was a bad one, discovered too late. It was built through underground springs which ever since have cascaded their surplus

Icicles formed in the frozen tunnel which were "as big as human bodies" in the long frozen winters of years ago. This was the view on 11 Janaury 2009, taken by P.Way volunteer Jon Bowers.

water down the vents and through the linings of the wall and roof – there was even a well above the tunnel. The West Hoathly end was the worst and, with freezing northwest winds blowing down through the portal, icicles 'as big as human bodies' stretched from roof to rail, necessitating track workers to knock them down before the passage of the first train in harsh winters.

In February 1954 an *East Grinstead Courier* correspondent talked to some gangers to view the removal of 100 tons of ice: "It was worse than this

in 1947," said one railwayman. "Then we had a ballast train in the tunnel of 49 trucks to move the ice from the tunnel and the shafts – and every one of them was full up."

Three of the five construction shafts were eventually blocked out, leaving two, capped by vast ventilation chimneys which remain today, on either side of the road through the centre of Sharpthorne up on the ridge. The tunnel was completed in 1881, a datestone encapsulated in the brickwork above each portal.

Far left: Trackbed cleared up to the tunnel on 18 November 1990.

Left: The south portal of Sharpthorne tunnel in March 1990, the route fenced off to inquisitors.

Below left: Ballast in place at the south portal in August 1991.

Below: Track was laid for convenience southwards through the tunnel from the engineering compound outstation at West Hoathly. Track was laid through the tunnel by December 1991.
ALL: MIKE ESAU

Arriving at West Hoathly

LSWR B4 *Normandy* and track gang arrive at West Hoathly on 5 March 1992.

Tracklaying work in the tunnel on 29 February 1992.

The extension gang mark the arrival of the North London Railway tank to the south portal of the tunnel on 29 February 1992, caused by the joining of the track from West Hoathly down to a point just south of the tunnel.

Left: The publican of the Bluebell Inn (right) toasts the arrival of the railway again (far right) at West Hoathly with Bluebell engineman (and fellow pub landlord!) Barry Cook. However, the Bluebell Inn is now closed and has since been converted to a private dwelling.

Left below: The first scheduled public train approaches West Hoathly on 17 April 1992 hauled by No 35027 Port Line, which was based at the railway at the time. A run-round loop was created just south of New Coombe Bridge, which was the extent of the operating line until the railway reached Kingscote two years later.

Below: Despite local residents initially being against the re-arrival of their railway, they deemed the presence of the line important enough to incorporate it into their village sign. COLIN TYSON

No 35027 *Port Line* waits to break the banner for the 'official opening' of the tunnel on 16 May 1992 at a ceremony performed by Sir Alastair Morton, chairman of Eurotunnel and Bluebell's Bernard Holden. ALL: MIKE ESAU

The Big Lift

by Peter Thomas

From BN Summer 1993

It is a delight to announce that the new bridge, carrying the railway over a local farm route, is now in place. This is the only new engineering works on the whole of the extension route, another of the many milestones for the railway and in particular a major step in our quest to reach East Grinstead.

The bridge was originally designed for assisting in the construction of the North Wales expressway, the improvement of the A55. It was used to receive rail-borne loads of aggregate. When that phase of road construction was completed it was spied in sidings at Llandudno Junction and Bluebell offered to purchase the five span bridge. Our bid had the advantage that we would take it when it was available and at short notice. The bridge spent some time at Horsted Keynes, indeed the remaining two spans stay for the moment in the field there, while three sections were transferred to the West Hoathly site.

Statutory approvals

Before the bridge could be used it was necessary to have its installation redesigned altogether with supporting structures. This entailed the railway proposals, overseen by an independent professional view, approved by the railway inspectorate and the county council – coupled with the normal planning approval. All this was successfully arranged by our project engineer, Steve Johnstone.

Installation

Some heavy rain in November and December 1992 delayed any hope of erecting the bridge at Christmas time. The centre piers had been in place for ages, with the outer abutments yet to be constructed.

Next, plans were laid to do the piling in February. Our construction team arranged holidays etc but alas two weeks before, the firm engaged went into liquidation. More frustration for Steve. A new firm was found and a new work week was arranged for late March. On day one, with the piles being drilled, a spring was struck! More delay, and it was almost the end of the week before the latest problems could be overcome. Rather than waste the team's 'working holiday' Steve decided to put the centre span in position using the crane which had already been booked.

With all the other work and concreting, all was ready for placing the bridge into place on 10 May. Steve was naturally a little tense. So many times, it seemed, his carefully laid plans had not come to fruition but this time everything went like clockwork. Precision engineering.

The day was not without its difficulties. When a span was placed on the piers last

Looking north at New Coombe on 21 February 1993, the central span piers for the bridge had been in position for a while.

The big lift underway, the crane being insured for £150,000.

Touching down carefully into position…

…and adjustments made to the deck.
ALL: MIKE ESAU

NEW COOMBE BRIDGE

February, that span was intended for the south position. Although the three spans are similar there are slight differences between them. And so to 10 May. The south span was lifted into place in the morning and rails were laid to enable the third span to be placed into position. LSWR B4 *Normandy*, under the careful control of driver Tom Dobson, pushed the third section on to the bridge and the crane lifted it over the last gap. Clearances were necessarily tight but in it went exact. The only problem was that the last span, originally intended for the centre spot, had one set of holes for the bolts slightly out of line. This was corrected afterwards.

At about 5pm that day, *Normandy* with a celebratory touch on the whistle, went on to the bridge right to the third (or northernmost) span. Well done Steve Johnstone and well done the construction gang who are all volunteers.

Cost

The end cost is looking like £43,000, a saving of £10,000 on the original estimate. This includes just over £10,000 for all professional overviews and design. If we had to go out to contract the likely cost of designing the bridge would have been somewhere between £30,000 and £50,000 and its construction in the order of £150,000.

A great day's work was celebrated on 10 May 1993 when, around 5pm, B4 *Normandy* went on to New Coombe Bridge with a celebratory whistle.
MIKE ESAU

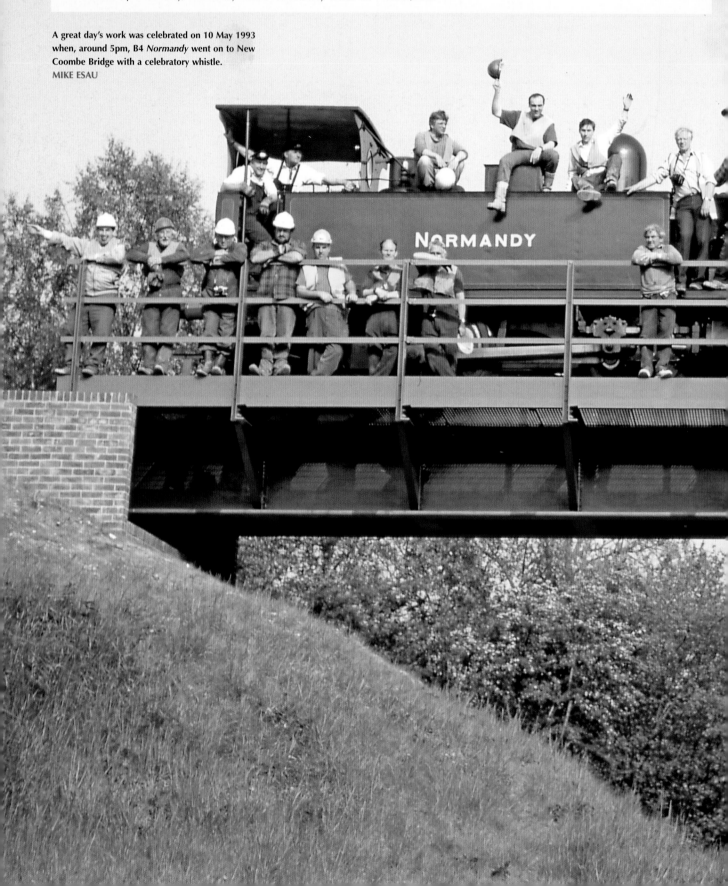

PHASE 4: NEW COOMBE

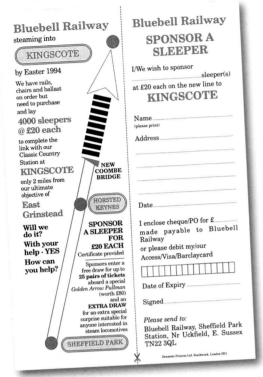

Bluebell Railway
steaming into

KINGSCOTE

by Easter 1994

We have rails,
chairs and ballast
on order but
need to purchase
and lay

**4000 sleepers
@ £20 each**

to complete the
link with our
Classic Country
Station at
KINGSCOTE
only 2 miles from
our ultimate
objective of

**East
Grinstead**

**Will we
do it?**

**With your
help - YES**

**How can
you help?**

NEW
COOMBE
BRIDGE

HORSTED
KEYNES

**SPONSOR
A SLEEPER
FOR
£20 EACH**
Certificate provided

Sponsors enter a
free draw for up to
25 pairs of tickets
aboard a special
Golden Arrow Pullman
(worth £80)
and an
EXTRA DRAW
for an extra special
surprise suitable for
anyone interested in
steam locomotives

SHEFFIELD PARK

**Bluebell Railway
SPONSOR A
SLEEPER**

I/We wish to sponsor
...................sleeper(s)

at £20 each on the new line to
KINGSCOTE

Name.................................
(please print)

Address.............................

....

....

....

Date....................................

I enclose cheque/PO for £..........
made payable to Bluebell
Railway
or please debit my/our
Access/Visa/Barclaycard

Date of Expiry.....................

Signed................................

Please send to:
Bluebell Railway, Sheffield Park
Station, Nr Uckfield, E. Sussex
TN22 3QL

Dramato Printers Ltd. Southwark, London SE1

'Sponsor a Sleeper' appeal leaflet, specifically designed to raise funds for sleepers for the section from New Coombe Bridge to Kingscote.

From Bluebell News

With trains now running through to just short of New Coombe Bridge, the summer of 1992 has seen the extension trackbed gang restarting its clearance work, moving south from the accommodation bridge at Mill Place Farm to link up with a similar party working northwards from the railhead at West Hoathly depot.

ENFORCEMENT

In May 1992 a meeting was called locally to deal with complaints the council had received from residents at West Hoathly and Sharpthorne.

There was a useful exchange of views in relation to operations in view of the pending planning application for a temporary loop to turn locomotives at West Hoathly, which the council had insisted upon. This was followed by the council officers putting before their June planning meeting, without any reference to the railway, a request that the railway had committed a clear breach of the 1985 approval conditions; and be instructed to remove access to the 'viewing area' or be served with an enforcement notice and taken before the magistrates court if the order is not complied with.

The 1985 condition 9 states there shall be no public access to the former station sites at West Hoathly and Kingscote (unless granted upon application). Following legal advice, the directors do not feel there has been a breach, but if there has been one, then the 'grace and favour' foot crossing provided for locals would also be a breach of the 1985 conditions, and the railway accordingly served notice on the parish council that in order to comply with the MSDC instruction it would close off the foot crossing from the end of July.

Of course this brought a number of protests to the council from local residents, resulting in the council agreeing to take no action – the railway in turn agreeing not to close the crossing.

A last look at the engineers' depot at the former cattle dock at West Hoathly, prior to the storage of materials transferring to the compound at East Grinstead.
PHIL BARNES

The rural idyll that is Birchstone Bridge, seen in the summer of 1992.
MICK BLACKBURN

Delivering ballast by dump truck to the railhead south of Birchstone Bridge in January 1994. MICK BLACKBURN

LSWR B4 *Normandy* on track laying duty south of Birchstone Bridge, spring 1994. MICK BLACKBURN

RAILS

There are two miles on to Kingscote from New Coombe Bridge and the railway has enough rail but needs £175,000 for ballast and sleepers. Trackbed clearance is progressing. The railway has to apply to WSCC about the footpath crossing the railway just north of Birch Farm nursery as it takes the view that the railway must apply to reinstate the stile which has not been required since the track was lifted. By early summer 1993 the engineers' base at West Hoathly had been moved to East Grinstead and the site at West Hoathly landscaped.

Still to finish at New Coombe Farm were the crossings and access roads and the diversion of a water pipe.

An application would have to be made to vary the original planning permission from the secretaries of state of 1985 to allow a stopping place at Kingscote. The railway is in discourse with local councillors in explaining its desire to return Kingscote to all its glory as a country station and the Kingscote team were aiming to get at least the Down platform wall in before track reaches the station.

It was announced that there would be a provisional programme to lay track to Deans Crossing over the weekend of 25-26 September 1993, and that ballast would be laid through the cutting to Ingwersens Nursery week commencing 11 October.

Apart from laying the track there was some accommodation works to attend to. Just south of Kingscote an 11kv power line crosses the railway and a stay wire close to the trackbed had to be moved slightly. Birch Farm foot crossing has been installed but winter weather has left the trackbed saturated in parts. Despite this, the single line up to Kingscote south points took just five weeks to lay! The south point was delivered on 9 March 1994, and the Midland Railway Centre's tamper worked south of Horsted Keynes on 14 March and came on to the new section later, thereby allowing tender engines to traverse the new section. The S&T Dept connected up the south points to the ground frame that had been removed from West Hoathly and finished on 18 April. An inspection by Major Poyntz took place the next day.

The first passenger train to Kingscote arrived on 23 April 1994.

Track laid south of Birchstone Bridge. MICK BLACKBURN

Boggy at Birchstone: It's a sea of mud for construction volunteers and their equipment during the winter of 1993-1994. MICK BLACKBURN

NEW COOMBE BRIDGE TO KINGSCOTE

Looking north towards Kingscote from Birchstone Bridge towards Mill Place in January 1994. MICK BLACKBURN

One load of ballast had to be dumped in order to retrieve another bogged-down dumper – delivering ballast south of Birchstone Bridge in January 1994. In three months' time, trains would be at Kingscote. MICK BLACKBURN

The trackbed near Mill Place Farm Bridge prior to the clearance of vegetation. MIKE ESAU

Deans Crossing

With the tree to the right as a reference point, a comparison looking north at Deans Crossing, between West Hoathly and Kingscote, on 8 August 1993 and with the railway in place on 29 August 1994 – a year later. BOTH: MIKE ESAU

The way north: the trackbed approximately a quarter-mile south of Kingscote. MIKE ESAU

The 'temporary' signal cabin at Kingscote (South) under construction. PETER TRIMMING

The new south point being installed at Kingscote on 17 March 1994, just a month before the public trains arrived. MIKE ESAU

Celebrity visiting locomotive GWR No 3440 *City of Truro* runs round the 1.17pm train to Sheffield Park at Kingscote at the southern point and Kingscote (South) cabin. PHIL BARNES

Extension people

Generally credited with 'getting the railway to Kingscote', Peter Thomas OBE, who sadly passed away on 2 January 1998 was generally 'Mr Extension' and every Sunday morning it could take him two hours to walk the length of Sheffield Park platform because of the amount of members that would want even the smallest snippet of extension news since they last saw him (no internet chat groups then!).

Bluebell's late president, Bernard Holden MBE. JON BOWERS

It was Peter's persuasive powers of negotiation that helped the railway no end when it came to dealing with landowners and stakeholders. Peter's project manager for the construction from Horsted Keynes to Kingscote was engineer Steve Johnstone.

After the railway had reached Kingscote, the project was managed for a while by Jim Turtle from the railhead at Kingscote and from the parcels van in the compound at East Grinstead.

It was soon becoming obvious that the next stages would need a project manager to bring all the infrasructure and administrative aspects together – and Bluebell volunteer locomotive driver Chris White was asked to take the role of infrastructure director in 2001. He brought a team of trustees and managers with varying responsibilities together for the common good of the railway. A consultant engineer with Atkins Rail, Croydon, it was to Chris that the railway looked to ultimately as project director, Northern Extension Project.

Chris had a good 'number two' in the form of infrastructure manager Matt Crawford, who brought with him a wide experience in several disciplines. Matt has been with Bluebell 'man and boy' as it were. Chris and Matt, together

with the volunteer team leaders and the army of project volunteers, should be thanked for all of their hard work and devotion to the cause at the 'cliff face'.

Finally, having chaired the founders' meeting of the society in 1959 and guided the railway through

NEP project manager and infrastructure director, Chris White. COLIN TYSON

some tough times, it was centenarian Bernard Holden MBE's final wish that he should be able to approach East Grinstead over the viaduct from the south – and preferably in the LBSCR saloon. That the saloon celebrates its centenary this year (2013) but has been out of traffic for more years than anyone remembers, is to the railway's eternal shame. However, Bernard did live to see the waste by road and waste by rail operations but sadly passed away aged 104 on 4 October 2012.

The Early Preservation Years
1985-1987

THE BLUEBELL EXTENSION RAILWAY LIMITED

Kingscote Station

Photos: R Bamberough

Will **YOU** help the Railway to buy it?

Kingscote station is for sale. The station buildings and offices are substantially intact as are the canopy, subway, up platform, dock and other features. Needless to say the station and its site are of vital strategic importance to our Extension project. We cannot afford to let the opportunity pass.

The offer includes the station, building, platform, trackbed and forecourt covering in all just over 3 acres and offers in excess of £80,000 are invited.

This is a considerable amount of money to raise. Our success depends upon your support. Please don't leave it to the other fellow!

Kingscote station on the market in 1984, contracts being exchanged early in 1985. R BAMBEROUGH. **Inset: the 1984 appeal leaflet.**

Kingscote was unquestionably a 'Barry-condition' station when purchased by Bluebell in January 1985 for a price in excess of £100,000. The building was basically in sound structural condition but had suffered from years of neglect and alterations. The down platform and buildings had been removed and the whole site was covered with saplings and mature trees, some over 40ft high which, 30 years previously, could have been dug out with a dinner fork.

It was a bitterly cold January when a small band of volunteers started work at weekends.

Conditions were inhospitable in the extreme! There was no water or electricity and nowhere for a fire to be lit as the grates had either been removed or smashed by vandals. Luckily no birds' nests blocked the chimneys so it was at least possible to light a fire with some old bricks forming a temporary grate. This didn't produce a great deal of heat but gave a comforting glow to accompany the candles. Tea was brewed with the aid of a primus stove and water was brought from Sheffield Park.

At some point an attempt had been made to convert the building into two or three

living units, so one can imagine the sinks and baths etc, accompanying pipe work and paraphernalia everywhere. The ladies WC and waiting room had been converted into a bathroom and kitchenette. On closer inspection of the gaping holes in the floor it was soon clear that not a single board, joist or wall plate was in sound condition. The waiting room window which faces the platform had been converted into a doorway leading to where there had been an extension. This had been removed prior to our purchase and the canopy had been allowed to sag – due

The hideous extension, first floor 'verandha' and those white-painted walls. R BAMBEROUGH

Slumbering and overgrown, the sight that awaited volunteers when first purchased. R BAMBEROUGH

Before the end of February 1985, the missing stanchion base had been dug out and the joists were being gradually eased back into place. Note the plinthed brickwork hacked away, the window to the Ladies' Waiting Room had become a door – and those white painted walls! R BAMBEROUGH

The Up platform subway steps, taken when the extension was still in place in early 1985. A raised manhole forming a step was between the subway and extension. R BAMBEROUGH

...to the missing stanchion also removed to accommodate the extension. The canopy was otherwise fairly intact. Some of the plinth brickwork had been hacked away to make it flush to the wall and this was hidden behind very poor rendering. The remainder of the face of the wall had been painted white.

The Gents WC and lamp room had been demolished with the exception of the wall facing onto the platform, still with its doorways but no doors. It is thought that this had been done to provide accommodation for two cars as the remnant of a 'car port' built from scrap materials was still in evidence. The main booking hall doors (both pairs) had been burned (fittings from them were found in the remains of an old bonfire) and replaced with pseudo Gothic oak panelled doors in frames fitted into the original frames. All that remained of the original fittings was a fitted bench seat in the booking hall and the ticket window. By some miracle the stained glass portions of all the booking hall windows and toplights remained in fair condition.

In the booking office there was a gaping hole in the wall where the fireplace used to be. Next to the chimney breast a doorway had been put through to join the hallway of the station house.

At the southern end, the walls dividing the porters room, coal store and original kitchen had been removed – along with the entire chimney breast. The doorway of the coal store had been bricked up to half its height and brickwork to one side of it removed along with the original stone lintel. An RSJ had then been substituted to form a wide window opening. On the platform there was the most hideous extension ever seen. This included the most technically impossible fireplace and chimney breast ever to be built. This part of the structure went through a hole in the canopy, cut for the purpose, not to mention holes in the brickwork to take joists, and once again, face brickwork painted white.

On the outside of the building on the platform side was a mass of soil and waste pipes from the bathrooms. Another doorway had been cut through the brickwork into what was the house coal store. In front of this doorway was a manhole which, for some

reason, was raised above the platform level and formed a step to the doorway.

Other than the SR concrete fencing on the up platform, all other fencing had been removed. The gate from the platform to the garden was just recognisable as a 1930s model complete with SR-marked hinges.

On the roof above the house entrance hall, a wooden structure had been built to serve as an observation platform which was accessed with some difficulty through the landing window. It is widely believed that this was for the male of the species to occupy whilst the other gender lazed on the side of the proposed swimming pool to be built into the trackbed. It was this proposal which required the total removal of the down platform and all the associated structures. Naturally, the proposal was dropped following this mass destruction! Other than the dilapidated well hut, the only evidence of any form of structure on the down side was the remains of the subway stairwell. This was filled with rubble and about half of the original steps remained; all the others and the platform brickwork having been pushed away.

In every room, peeling plaster, paint and ripped out electricity cables vied with each other to form festoons.

The first visits to Kingscote in the horrible weather immediately after purchase were spent

assessing the situation and wondering what to do; once somebody picked up a paint scraper and started on a wall it was obvious! It was thought prudent to give all the woodwork a quick coat of Southern colours for protection and let the world see a nicer looking 'Bluebell' station. This 'quick lick of paint' and hacking back undergrowth took quite a few weeks, during which time volunteer attendance grew and more jobs were started.

By February 1985 the floor in the ladies waiting room had been mended and the missing stanchion replaced, after gentle, prolonged jacking up of the canopy. March saw an invasion from the Bluebell's Croydon Area Group, who tackled a lot of muck clearing tasks which included removal of bricks and rubbish from the subway.

By this time, the various authorities had reconnected the water and electricity, at least to the distribution points, so life was much more comfortable for all.

The 'Kingscote Saga' had started. Almost like a disease it spread until a regular team transpired. A tea fund was set up which produced a few pounds profit to buy bits and pieces. This was supplemented as more and more society members got to hear about the work, and came to visit on Sundays and made small donations to assist the funding. As the donations grew so the projects became more ambitious.

The author (bending over, right) and others tackling the down side subway. The top of the arch was exposed and any reclaimable bricks were salvaged. A futher five courses of bricks were taken down before rebuilding started. R BAMBEROUGH

July 1986 and the bricked up doorway to the extension (right) and the coal store doorway half bricked up to a window. The old lintel had to be removed, hence being jacked up. A new concrete moulded lintel is in place.
MALCOLM PORTER

Plinth brickwork being reinstated, which has reached as far north as the ladies' window. The void in the gents' and lamp room is also shown. R BAMBEROUGH

The 'quick lick' paint job had now graduated to a proper job of stripping and progressing through the various stages of painting. This naturally means that steps were retraced.

By May the carpentry in the ladies WC had been started and rewiring commenced upstairs. April saw a start on renovating the down side subway stairwell. This required a lot of digging to expose the remaining sound brickwork. Many courses of brickwork had also to be removed owing to frost damage (in the mortar joints). These bricks were cleaned and stacked along with those removed from the subway infill for re-use. Eight thousand bricks would be required to rebuild the stairwell, plus sand, cement etc. There was about £40 in the fund and we had about 1,000 usable bricks. Hands went into pockets and soon a 10-ton load of sand was delivered, along with bags of cement. For the bricks, it was decided to rescue some from the derelict site of West Hoathly station – an arduous process which continued throughout most of the remaining months of 1985.

Car boots and a Land Rover were employed as transport; about 30 bricks being enough weight for the average boot. To rescue 7,000 or so was amazing. They had to be removed from an existing wall and carried some 150 yards to be loaded. Once unloaded at Kingscote they were removed from the forecourt, through the station and across the trackbed to the site. This was all achieved

The last job of 1986 was fabricating a new sill to the Ladies Waiting Room window, formerly a doorway. MALCOLM PORTER

because of the enthusiasm of a lot of people, although the actual reconstruction was carried out by only a few.

It was decided that the copings would be reproduced in concrete, the original stone ones being smashed during demolition. A mould was made and one section of coping (50in) was produced per week – each with two tapered holes to anchor the handrail stanchions. The original stanchions were still available, as in earlier years they had been acquired by some forward-thinking members (when the stairwell was demolished) and stored at Horsted Keynes. Of the 22 stanchions only one of these cast iron items got broken. A pattern was produced and a local foundry cast a replacement for us, paid for privately. By the end of December the stairwell was finished except for the top four steps.

Water was percolating through the subway brickwork and flooding the subway. Later investigation revealed unfinished drain work and 12 feet of pipe missing under the platform. Work on the stairwell was halted and shovels used to expose the problem. New pipes were laid and manholes inserted to ensure free flow of the storm water. This work took several weeks as some of the digging was quite close to the nasty extension on which demolition had started. By the end of July the drain work was complete and the demolition of the extension finished.

Work had been continuing internally. The bare booking office was starting to look resplendent once again thanks to the acquisition of redundant fittings. Elegance was the order of the day with built in drawers complete with brass handles and mahogany worktop (from Tunbridge Wells West) and an LBSCR safe arrived ex-Southwater – the key for which was still hanging in Horsham booking office!

An odd door and parts of wood mouldings etc came from Southwater and Polegate. Subway handrail brackets of LBSCR pattern were rescued from Polegate and we had

enough genuine benches for both platforms.

Rewiring continued until soon we had a cooker working and were able to use an electric kettle. An old Rayburn which had been donated was also fitted and plumbed in, so by early 1986 we had hot water as well.

Originally, the well/pump house was at the bottom of an embankment behind the down platform but subsequent dumping of spoil on this site had almost buried the hut. The roof, however, was still visible. A lot of this spoil was removed by a gang of venture scouts from West Wickham and the pumping equipment has since been removed for future restoration. Due to the generosity of the Croydon Area Group, the hut roof was felted, battened and retiled with reclaimed tiles.

The removal of tree roots and saplings etc was an ongoing job throughout 1985 as was the resurrection of the flower borders. Some of Mr Ward's famous old briars were found and still produce fine roses to this day.

An elderly chap turned up in 1985 and took on the task of cleaning the old paint off the mullions, sills and lintels to reveal the original stone. This entailed hours and hours of rubbing with pumice week after week – such a menial task but the results were magnificent.

Towards the latter end of 1985 a start had been made to reconstruct the forecourt fence, this being done with the aid of reclaimed materials. 1986 started with re-routing the soil and waste pipes serving the first floor (which was now occupied by a 'Bluebell caretaker'). Once connected to the new double sealed internal manhole created for the purpose, the ugly pipes on the platform side were disconnected and removed. This left several holes in the walls and one in the canopy. The 'raised' manhole was also decommissioned, making way for us to brick up the offending doorway and repair the brickwork where the extension was tied in. This work required a quantity of red Victorian facing bricks and 1,000 were delivered for £300.

The subway steps were finished by about March leaving the re-pointing, handrail and recently-discovered blocked drainage to be sorted out. As work progressed other problems came to light: the chimneys needed repointing and the ridge tiles were coming adrift. It was decided to repair the roof without delay. The previously mentioned 'gallery' was useful in gaining access to the main roof to carry out the repairs, which were done with relative ease.

Repairs to the canopy south end also began in 1986. One section required complete removal and reinstatement to replace some rot where timber met brickwork. The gutters were removed, renovated and replaced. Obtaining a fall on the gutter was a little difficult as the century old canopy was perhaps not quite as straight as it was, but it all looks superb. It was a good year for paintwork as Kingscote qualified for a grant from Dulux and the 1930s rendering was dealt with.

The original stanchion bases were excavated on the down side, along with a small length of the original platform brickwork, and prepared for reconstruction.

The very last job of 1986 was to cast a concrete sill for the waiting room window. This required a mould to be made to accommodate all the awkward angles which had been carved in stone originally. The concrete remained in the mould for several weeks, well protected from the frost. When turned out of the mould in early February, much to our relief, it was an excellent result.

The Ladies WC was also tackled, the plaster work being carried out along with carpentry and plumbing work, with two functioning WCs and a hand basin.

When the now fairly rotten observation platform was removed, it revealed that the roof underneath required repair. On closer inspection it was found to be in a very poor state and required a complete strip down. The tiles were removed and sorted, and second hand tiles obtained to replace the damaged ones. Once the old battens had been removed it was clear that woodworm had got a grip of the timbers, over half of which had to be replaced using second hand materials. Everything was treated before re-assembly, then felted and battened.

At that point, the gents toilet still had to be rebuilt, needing at least 4,000 facing bricks, plus lots of other materials. The down side was still bare, requiring a platform and a canopy, a signal box and fences…and we were four years away from when we hoped the first trains would arrive.

ADDENDUM
This article was written in early October 1987 and was intended for publication in *Steam Railway*. Whilst it has been condensed and altered for this publication, and to try to ensure that the chronology is about right, there may be errors, but I am happy that it reflects the general situation for the first two and three quarter years of Kingscote as a Bluebell station.

I have deliberately omitted names as many people were involved at the time, although only few were involved with the major works, as a whole much was achieved because of the unified efforts of many.

I left the railway shortly after this time due to personal reasons. In recent months, and now retired, I have been catching up with events at Kingscote and the railway in general

This LBSCR handbill advertising 'Eridge Hunt Steeplechases on Easter Monday' was folded and used as packing material behind a hinge to one of the reclaimed ex-Polegate doors.

via my computer at home in Lincolnshire. The changes at Kingscote are fantastic to say the very least. It pays tribute to all those who continued the work there, and makes me feel very proud to have been involved at all. The jewel in the Bluebell crown.

Because I was heavily involved may I make just one observation. Modern handrail brackets have been used on the downside stairwell. This is anathema to my efforts, as, in addition to the work at Kingscote, I spent many hours at Polegate cutting out the LBSCR handrail brackets from the brickwork with a club hammer and cold chisel, followed by many days restoring them all for reuse at Kingscote. These were left at Kingscote and if they are still stored somewhere, I would consider it an honour to fit them where they should be. This, to me, would finish off the excellent work properly. Just an appropriate profile of handrail would then be required, not too far out of the realms of possibility?

MALCOLM D PORTER

The spring of 1986 and the author's wife, Pat, and the late Wyn Thomas man the tea urn for a fundraising day. Malcolm Porter

Replacement subway hand rail stanchion. Malcolm Porter

The early 1990s

by John Sisley

The following details have been obtained from reports featured in 'Friends of Kingscote' Newsletters 12, 13, 14 and 15 published in 1992. Reference was also made to *Bluebell News* of 1992 and early 1993. During 1992, the line was still being constructed from New Coombe Bridge to Kingscote. The FoK Newsletters reported on both work on the station building (and its surrounds) and on the trackbed from New Coombe Bridge to Kingscote. This synopsis, in the main, concentrates on work carried out at Kingscote.

John Reynard was responsible for all four 'Restoration Reports'. These reports summarised many aspects of work being conducted at the Kingscote station building. They form the basis of the following record of achievements during 1992.

The gentlemen's toilet was worked on throughout the year. All the underground pipework for the toilets and sink drains was completed. The foul water drains were tested successfully. However, three leaks were discovered close to an adjacent manhole and were dealt with. The local building inspector was asked to visit the site and approve the work. He asked for one thing to be altered, which was done, and on a subsequent visit passed the works. Blockwork up to windowsill height at the back and two further courses up at the front were laid. Mid Sussex Water installed and connected a water meter to supply the new toilet block. Andy Stadden was responsible for reporting on this project.

Richard Barton wrote that the Up side canopy was subject to a great deal of work during 1992. During the repairs, a railway delivery note was found concealed on the underside of the lead gutter. This was dated 18 April 1919 – which gave the impression that no major

Kingscote, October 1985. The station had been in Bluebell ownership for a year and was just starting the process of back-converting from some horrible 'additions and improvements' by previous owners. MIKE ESAU

repairs had taken place since that date.

The main concerns were the glazed portion of the canopy at the north end which had started to sag and the gutter timbers were completely rotten. All the existing glass had to be replaced with wire safety panels (this was a legal/safety requirement). Sid Sutton was responsible for installing a new lead gutter – his last gutter job had been at Danehill Church. Three new glazing frames were made by two ex-Horsted Keynes carpenters using real joints with wedges and dowels, no screws or nails. New glazing bars were made using the C&W Dept's circular saw, band saw and spindle moulder. A new downpipe was added at the north end of the canopy. Les Haines made the moulding to replace a missing section from the base of the most southern of the canopy supports.

Most members of the Kingscote team were involved in some way with the repairs and the repainting of this major project.

In the spring the clearance gang was diverted to help with lineside clearance and fencing work between Horsted House Farm and the south end of the tunnel. This, it is assumed, was to prepare the railway for the inspection by Major Olver on 14 April and the official opening through the tunnel the following month.

In April, the station was entered for the Association of Railway Preservation Society's Ian Allan Railway Heritage Awards. Kingscote won the *Railway World* award for 'incomplete schemes showing the most promise'. A plaque and a grant of £1,000 was presented to John Reynard by the Duke of Gloucester at the Royal Society of Arts on 24 November 1992. John was accompanied by Michael Heathcote and Andy Stadden.

Over Easter the hanging tiles on the forecourt side of the station were removed. It was reported that many were hanging on by a wing and a prayer. During the removal a rather pleasing moulding of an urn of flowers was revealed in the original rendering. The rendering was unpainted but the wooden frames and the flowers appeared to have been painted in dark red. The tiles appeared to be hand-made. Fortunately not many breakages were suffered so the majority of them were cleaned and rehung. After much discussion it was decided to replace the tiles over the original rendering. New treated battens were fitted. Two hundred new scalloped and 15 pairs of angled

Home is where the hearth is: It's January 1991 and the booking hall has a welcoming fire for the benefit of volunteers and any impromptu visitors. MIKE ESAU

tiles were purchased from a local merchant. They proved to be a very good match with the original ones. They cost £326 with another £30 for the tile battens.

Tom Simcock wrote four very detailed reports entitled Extension Update. It is interesting to read that the line north to West Hoathly passed inspection by Major PM Olver OBE on 14 April 1992. The inspection train was hauled by No 35027 *Port Line*.

Kingscote's platforms under construction. The Down platform was missing completely and the Up platform north of the former toilet block likewise.
MICK BLACKBURN

Bluebell locomotive driver and master bricklayer Freeland Eastwood at work on the ramp at the north end of the Up platform. MICK BLACKBURN

On 28 June a fundraising sponsored walk took place. This was organised by Les Haines who had spent four weekends walking the local footpaths preparing a nine mile and a five mile route. In total over 100 people registered for the event. Andy Stadden gave a detailed report on his day – 81 people sponsored Andy raising £1,188. The total amount raised was over £4,400 – compared with £6,600 in 1991 and £4,930 in 1993.

Towards the end of the year the overhead electricity supply had been removed and replaced by an underground cable. It was fortunate that a groundwork contractor was working in the area and needed somewhere to store his plant overnight. In return for providing space he agreed to dig a trench from the electricity pole at the roadside to the station building. Within a day Seeboard delivered a 50-metre length of ducting which the groundwork contractor laid in the trench and covered over. Later Seeboard installed the cable.

British Telecom laid ducts from a new joint box close to the road to the station. This also provided a new route to the nearby cottages, thus removing the overhead lines where they crossed the trackbed south of the station.

During the year all the lamp posts on the Up platform had lanterns fitted including the glass. These lanterns were produced by Murray Scott (the father of C&W employee Sheina Foulkes). Murray wrote an article entitled New Lamps for

Down platform canopy under construction.

Old which appeared in Newsletter 13. This gave a very comprehensive account of the work involved.

Ralph Olesen helped to locate the surface water pipes around the site using a rather sophisticated drain detector. A pipe was found about 60ft from the building in the goods yard.

John Foulkes wrote a very interesting article on

the decorating of the booking hall which covered work before and during 1992. Major work had started in 1988 when the ceiling was reported 'to be accelerating into shabbiness'. It was a constant battle to maintain a fine decorative order in a building that is damp, destabilised and unoccupied most of the time.

The choice of paint colours became a matter of

Trains are just a few months away from arriving here, even if the trackbed is more representative of a canal. MIKE ESAU

Bluebell president Bernard Holden MBE and his wife Lilian are met by Kingscote stationmaster Alan Closs on opening day, 23 April 1994. DAVID MARK

The gent's toilet block was a complete reconstruction, which had reached window level by February 1993. MIKE ESAU

The tedious but necessary work of fencing by Friends of Kingscote volunteers. MIKE ESAU

A gem of a rural station, seen in April 2008. Much hard work went into its restoration. COLIN TYSON

serious debate. The old flooring was removed and replaced. In 1992 a local plasterer made good where necessary on the walls and ceiling in the waiting room (for a charge of £205); he did a very good job which enabled inside work for the winter months. Work continued on the renovation of the fireplace. The old paint was stripped off to reveal the original slate finish, which was then polished. The long timber seat situated under the window was original but needed two new legs. Professional help was being sought to repair the fireplaces in the waiting room and also the booking hall.

The forecourt fencing was repainted. It was last painted five years previously and was looking rather tatty. Lewis Norris, a new member, painted the platform seats.

Steve Johnstone managed to obtain sufficient fence posts for about 400 yards of fencing on the Down side. Ron Harwood busied himself clearing the fenceline to enable this work to be completed.

Les Haines carried out an extensive survey of the whole site. From his results, both the boundaries and levels were defined. A start could now be made on the trackwork drawing.

Michael Heathcote spent a great deal of time working on the Permanent Way hut close to the stone overbridge, south of Kingscote. He mended/replaced windows, changed the door and rebuilt the chimney. It was suggested that he was building his retirement home which was quickly denied. A visiting scout group from Croydon camped on the trackbed and used this Permanent Way hut as a base while carrying out considerable clearance of the cutting.

The stationmaster's garden was maintained by the weekend volunteers. String beans, tomatoes, courgettes, marrows and herbs were reported to be successful crops. A later report mentioned that the vegetable garden had been built up with topsoil from the trackbed and parsnips, beetroot, spinach, onions and Jerusalem artichokes had been added to the list of vegetables planted. Geoff and Janet Tarrant were attending to other parts of the gardens.

John Foulkes gave details on a meeting held on 27 September 1992, 'to discuss the needs of Kingscote station in the run-up to its opening as a terminus'. Several items were covered. Peter Thomas announced that the company would, that winter, be seeking permission for a change of use of the Kingscote building to that of a railway station. It was stated at this meeting that Kingscote's ethos as a country station would be respected.

A list of some magnitude was produced by Roger Barton in November showing all restoration work still to be carried out at Kingscote. A staggering 48 jobs were listed – many of which were of a substantial nature.

In November, Roger Barton and John Reynard spent a week with the Extension Company's JCB pulling out tree roots and digging a rough ditch close to Milepost 14½.

Plans for the reconstruction of the Down platform were discussed. Planning permission would be required for the platform walls. It was estimated that 60,000 bricks would be needed, at a cost of £7000 (plus sand and cement). David Willis produced a preliminary drawing for the Down platform front. A bricklayer from

Friends of Kingscote membership currently stands at £220, with an annual subscription of £12.

If you would like to become a member please contact Mary Sisley, membership secretary at mary@johnandmary.waitrose.com or write to her c/o Friends of Kingscote, Kingscote Station, Vowels Lane, East Grinstead, West Sussex RH19 4LD.

Your support would be very much appreciated and will help to continue to maintain Bluebell's 'country' station and its surroundings.

within the membership was urgently sought and the post was ably filled by loco driver and craftsman bricklayer Freeland Eastwood. The subway walls were painted using white cellar paint.

It was recorded in *Bluebell News* that FoK membership stood at £350 (subscription £12 per year).

A final note – the writer echoes the thoughts of our present FoK volunteers who realise how much we owe to those who worked so arduously in the pioneering days. With work starting in 1985 and the first Bluebell Railway passenger train arriving on 23 April 1994 (St George's Day), the volunteers achieved much in eight years at their northern outpost, separated from the rest of their railway but united by a common bond – to see trains back through Kingscote and onto East Grinstead.

Above: The cabin structure of the signalbox at the north end of the Down platform at Kingscote was formerly Brighton Upper Goods signalbox. BRIAN HYMAS

Left: The brick base under construction in July 1996. MICK BLACKBURN

Below Left: The signalbox 'top' is craned into position on 30 August 1996. MIKE ESAU

Below: Jubilant Friends of Kingscote volunteers. MIKE ESAU

Public re-opening

SECR C Class No 592 arrives at Kingscote with the 10am train from Sheffield Park as the first public train on re-opening of the station, Saturday 23 April 1994.
MIKE ESAU

The 'official' opening of Kingscote station came on 21 May 1994 and No 592 once again did the honours, this time specially decorated in LBSCR style as it breaks the banner to re-open the station and the latest section of the northern extension. IAN WRIGHT

PHASE 5:
KINGSCOTE TO IN

2002-2010

O nce Bluebell had reached Kingscote in 1994 it was time for the railway's management to take stock. It was tantalisingly only two miles from its ultimate destination of East Grinstead and yet it might as well be a whole world away. The bus link that the railway provided from East Grinstead station to Kingscote station, firstly on operating days and latterly on high days and holidays, proved popular with those visitors arriving by train at East Grinstead from the north. The bus link was provided partly for this link and partly because local planning restrictions forbade the use of public car parking at Kingscote.

Peter Thomas, the man always directly quoted by Bluebell volunteers as 'the man who got us to Kingscote' had now sadly passed away and it seemed that much of the 'pioneering' impetus had gone. Jim Turtle led a team working from the luggage van base at East Grinstead but it has to be borne in mind that at that time the railway still didn't own all the land required between Kingscote and East Grinstead; there were still uncertainties over our station site land at East Grinstead and the fact that the railway couldn't yet raise further funds (via a third share issue) for land that it didn't then own.

Sign 'commemorating commencement' of this stage of construction. MIKE ESAU

The buffer stop looking north at Kingscote, with trackbed vegetation cleared behind, on 14 May 2003. MIKE ESAU

Right: Looking south along the course of the trackbed at the 15½ milepost at Hazelden in 2000. MIKE ESAU

Looking north towards the south end of Imberhorne Tip from Hazelden Farm. MIKE ESAU

Speaking in *Bluebell News Spring 2002*, plc chairman Graham Flight reviewed the situation north of Kingscote.

Following the purchase of the western half of the trackbed immediately north of Kingscote, we are able to construct the railway on that part of the formation and subject to the finalisation of negotiations in respect of Imberhorne Tip and East Grinstead station site, this has meant that we have effectively 'joined up' Kingscote to East Grinstead. We are currently looking at how we can 'make a start' by laying track north of the Kingscote buffer stops. If you consider the land now in our ownership and the objectors to the Public Inquiry back in 1983, this is a major achievement.

LIGHT RAILWAY ORDER

Although the original LRIO expired on 31 December 2001, we were advised not to seek renewal prior to that expiry. Although the LRO has expired, we are able to continue with construction work and it is only once the line has been fully rebuilt that we need formal permission to operate the train service. This will be under a Transport & Works Act Order which we believe may take some two years in process.

Bluebell volunteer locomotive driver Chris White had been asked to take the role of Infrastructure Director in 2001 and brought a team of trustees and managers with varying responsibilities together for the common good of

Above and Below: Looking south, back towards Kingscote, from the vicinity of Hazelden Farm on 14 May 2003. MIKE ESAU

the railway. A consultant engineer with Atkins Rail, Croydon, it was to Chris that the railway looked to as project director, Northern Extension Project.

ASH LEA FARM

Bluebell News Autumn 2002. Debris has been cleared from the formation of the dam that was previously at this location. The bulk of the sludge that had been in the water behind the dam has now been removed. In recent weeks a start has been made on excavating the waste dumped on the trackbed that was purchased from Ash Lea Farm. This will take

Drainage works on the up side at Hazelden. **MIKE ESAU**

Culvert at Hazelden. The wording 'FOK 2004' is noted in the cement. MIKE ESAU

Aside from clearance work and reinstating the 'permanent way' there are other matters to attend to in reconstruction such as water courses, drains and culverts. The original water course at Hazelden is exposed. **MIKE ESAU**

The smart occupation bridge at Hazelden. MIKE ESAU

some time as it comprises a mixture of soil, scrap metal and general farm waste.

Bluebell News Autumn 2003. Tracklaying from Kingscote to Imberhorne Lane started in early September 2003. This section is now designated a works construction site and access is only for authorised persons.

Mayor of East Grinstead Beverley Heasman unveiled a commemorative board on 29 October 2003 to mark the start of the final phase and BR No 80151 made its way north over the newly laid sections of track, driven by Ian Wright.

Bluebell News Autumn 2004. A single line railway has now been constructed from the hand points north of Kingscote station to the infill which occupies the cutting south of Imberhorne Lane Bridge. About a mile in length, this comprises flat bottom rail on concrete sleepers laid in deep ballast. Protected by locked gates and catch points at the south end, this is technically an engineers siding worked by special operating arrangements approved by HMRI.

The standard of workmanship is very high. Not only does the track look professional but the efforts that have gone into core activities such as fencing, drainage, cable routing and vegetation clearance are a credit to everyone.

Loco men Terry Cole and Tony Drake bring LSWR B4 *Normandy* and a ballast train to Hazelden on 27 July 2004. MIKE ESAU

The people that make it happen: Our loco crew take a mid-day break with the extension workers at Hazelden on 27 July 2004. MIKE ESAU

"We filled in Hil

by Derek Thorogood

In the early part of the 20th century, East Grinstead Urban District Council installed a refuse incinerator on land, formerly a brickworks, between Durkin Road and the railway line at St Margaret's Junction. It was one of those familiar red brick buildings with their tall chimneys which Messrs Heenan & Froude designed for authorities all across Britain. The theory was splendid but I guess that maintaining the furnaces in good order and keeping smoke nuisance to a minimum were severe difficulties, and, by the time I joined the council as an articled pupil in 1941, burning had been abandoned. The council then used the land there for tipping, no doubt filling any old clay pits that still remained. Today the land is part of the Charlwoods Road Industrial Area.

The council's engineer during the war was HC Golding, and his deputy was FCC Wood (in this

piece I shall use the term 'engineer' for the council's chief technical officer, although the title was interchangeable with 'surveyor', and 'Engineer & Surveyor'). FCC Wood was a giant of a man, and a christian gentleman. He taught me much. I left East Grinstead in 1948 and served local authorities in Surrey until 1967.

The council had an establishment further down the line – adjoining Hill Place Cutting. This was the High Grove Isolation Hospital, for patients from East Grinstead and the surrounding area suffering from infectious diseases such as scarlet fever. It had four single-storey blocks, each with two wards, and I reckon matron could get anything from four to eight beds in a ward, depending on how tight she packed them. One of these blocks is still standing. There was also an admin building and nurses' quarters. The hospital stood on a triangle of land with the Imberhorne Lane bridge at the south point, Imberhorne Lane to the west, the railway cutting to the east, and the

fields of Hill Place Farm along the north side.

Gradually the hospital fell out of use. I suppose the isolation of patients and advances in medicine made those virulent diseases more and more rare. I believe it was barely used for its original purpose during the war.

One day, about 1966, FCC Wood, still keeping the show running as deputy engineer, was at the south end of the site, searching for the old hospital's cesspool. He found it all right as he had the great misfortune to fall into it. Happily, his shouts for help were eventually heard and he was rescued. But he never fully recovered, and he reluctantly retired on health grounds. In 1967 I took over his post.

When I returned to East Grinstead, the town was expanding fast and the council was using a field at Hill Place Farm for waste disposal. This was nearing its limit, and the railway cutting close by was a splendid opportunity for what I think today would be called 'constructive landfill'.

Place Cutting"

If my memory is right, the council had by then bought the cutting, and a planning application was in the pipeline. None of us then conceived that what the railway heroes were doing down at Sheffield Park and Horsted Keynes had any bearing on our activities.

So tipping started, in early 1968. Access was from Imberhorne Lane, across the old hospital site, and down a ramp made in the west side of the cutting. The general plan was that household waste would go in the centre and south end of the cut, while inert waste, such as builders' rubbish, went in at the north end.

For most of the time I was there, my chief was Tony Kilby, who came to East Grinstead from Chertsey. He was a great lad, and an enthusiast for the pulverisation of domestic refuse. He guided the council to the purchase of a 'Tollemache' pulveriser. This reduced the volume of refuse, and so extended the life of the cutting as a tip. It made refuse easier to handle but less

attractive to rats and insects, and it avoided the requirement to spread nine inches of inert material over each day's work.

The Tollemache pulveriser was housed in a new building at the north end of the hospital site. It was commissioned in 1970. It consisted of a fixed vertical steel cylinder through which ran a central shaft driven by an electric motor. On the shaft were mounted steel hammers, rather smaller than brick-sized, pivoted at the shaft. When the shaft turned rapidly, the hammers swung outwards to almost touch the steel casing. Refuse fed in at the top of the cylinders passed all these flying blocks of steel on its way to the bottom, and got thoroughly knocked about as it went. It came out at the bottom almost crumb-like, and passed up a conveyor belt to fill a large tipper lorry. The loaded lorry was driven down into the cutting for tipping. We used a bulldozer-like machine for spreading and consolidation.

Ken Cross ran the plant and drove the lorry and

Looking south towards the north end of the tip at Hill Place Farm Bridge on 22 August 1998.
MIKE ESAU

the tractor. One of his jobs was to weld new metal on to worn hammers. The reader will guess that 100 tons of waste passing down the cylinder each week would cause a deal of wear and tear on the hammers. It did. Rebuilding the hammers was a substantial element in the running costs.

The machine was quite noisy, although I do not recall any serious complaint on that score. What we did get were complaints of flies in a nearby house. That was burdensome for the occupiers and a disappointment for us. While I was there, we never really overcame that problem.

As the cutting filled, the trees growing on its sides had to be felled. Near the bottom the sides were steep and rocky. Two thirds of the way up, there were level strips along both sides, wide enough for a lorry. At the top the banks sloped at around 45°. I thought that this strange

"WE FILLED IN HILL PLACE CUTTING"

cross-section was probably because the old navvies, digging down from ground level, hit sandstone earlier than their engineer expected, and so he was able to reduce the width they had to dig out.

While the cutting was filling, the council had to look for the next hole in the ground that would be good to fill. We finally decided to go for St Margaret's Loop, the old railway cutting that had taken Tunbridge Wells West-bound trains from the Oxted line to East Grinstead high level station. It had some of the advantages of Hill Place Cutting, but its disadvantage, of course, was that it was by no means isolated. Many houses had gardens running down to its edge. To offset that, we planned to make the pulverised refuse into compost while it was still at High Grove, and then, after it had matured, truck it to the loop. The residents of East Grinstead were unconvinced that this would be a good thing (and with hindsight, who would blame them?). There was a public inquiry, and the inspector's decision went against us. So another scheme bit the dust.

By then the re-organisation of local government was approaching. Waste disposal became a county council responsibility, and I moved to inflict a waste disposal plan on the citizens of East Sussex. East Grinstead became part of West Sussex, whose council completed the filling of the cutting.

Different engineers have different ideas, and I believe the pulveriser at High Grove dropped out of use about that time. I have lost touch, but I understand East Grinstead's waste now ends up at Warnham, near Horsham.

(Speaking in 2001) Derek said: "It must now be approaching 30 years since the last refuse was tipped there. The decomposition that goes on in the early years after tipping is probably complete by now, although I expect a musty smell will linger when a fresh section of tip is first opened. It will not be unbearable, and I hope the excavation goes ahead without difficulty.

"One of my dearest wishes is to survive to see a steam locomotive coming through that cutting and over the viaduct into East Grinstead station. Even if my grandchildren have to wheel me there."

Tip top: Looking south at the southern end of the tip at the parapet of Imberhorne Lane Bridge, where a tree clearance gang are working on 7 February 1998. MIKE ESAU

Hill Place Farm Bridge

Imberhorne Lane Bridge

Clay Capping starts here.

The infilled cutting at Imberhorne in 1995, stretching from the Southern side of Imberhorne Lane Bridge to Hill Place Farm Bridge, both bridges parapets only being visible at track level. PHILIP LANE PHOTOGRAPHY

Testing the Tip

A total of 13 trial pits, of one metre square and up to 13.5 metres deep, were dug along the centre line of Imberhorne Tip in late November/early December 1997. Below the clay capping material, which is 2.5m deep, the infill consists mostly of domestic waste comprising a mixture of 40% plastic, 15% fabric, 15% paper and cardboard, 5% glass and 5% metal in a silt/clay mix. The remainder of the infill is made up of builders' rubble, mostly at the south end; old tyres and a small amount of scrap metal towards the north end.

With the exceptiion of some asbestos sheeting, no other hazardous substances have been found and the amount of methane gas is also quite low. However, the tip is still active with a strong odour and steam is rising from a number of trial pits (and it's not a C2X locomotive!)

Anecdotal information has suggested that many old army vehicles had been buried at the north end of the tip. Although no evidence of these has been found during the excavation of the trial pits, the following items have been: track ballast at the bottom of trial pit No 2, two water tanks, a metal bath, a porcelain toilet, various car parts, a complete washing machine, a newspaper dated 1969 and a milk churn – the contents of which were tested!

This all adds up to good news as the results confirm that removal should be relatively straightforward and allows final planning for the excavation of the tip to proceed. A detailed quote from a waste consortium is expected soon which will include options of removal by rail or road.

Bluebell News Spring 1998.

Trial boring at Imberhorne Tip on 1 December 1997. BOTH: MIKE ESAU

Clay capping
Nibbling the elephant

From Bluebell News, Summer 2005.

Monday 6 June 2005 became D-Day as the first of Imberhorne Tip's clay capping spoil trains were brought to the site to remove excavated soil.

The material, dumped to the south of Imberhorne Lane, is being taken by train to reinstate part of the formation on the Ardingly Spur at Horsted Keynes – removed when Sheriff Mill Viaduct was demolished.

The daily spoil trains are mainly being hauled by visiting Ivatt 2-6-2 tank No 41312 and it is expected that over 100 train movements will be required to remove the 18,000 cubic metres of material. The total tip capacity is 130,000 cubic yards, of which 96,000 comprise the domestic waste.

Only two Grampus wagons were ready for service by 6 June but the trainload will be strengthened in the near future, including a Turbot wagon borrowed from the Lavender Line.

Right: Local households were leafleted regarding the proposals to remove spoil by road, giving information about hours of operation and preferred routes etc.

Visiting Ivatt tank No 41312 has propelled its two wagons and a brake van to the south end of the tip at Imberhorne and the wagons are being filled with clay capping for transfer to the Ardingly Spur on 7 June 2005. JON BOWERS

The Ivatt takes its two wagons south through Kingscote on 6 June 2005.
ANDREW STRONGITHARM

Bluebell News Autumn 2005 declares the good news about there being a bridge underneath there! JON BOWERS

Aerial view, now showing the exposed bridge at Imberhorne Lane, which can be compared with the view on page 73. PHILIP LANE PHOTOGRAPHY

Above: More capping removal under way in the Spring of 2009, with duties undertaken by visiting Class 73 locomotive *Perseverance*. JON BOWERS

Left: Standing on the top of the tip looking south at the excavated clay capping on 9 May 2008. STEPHEN FAIRWEATHER

Above: *Perseverance* and its wagons at Horsted Keynes on 30 January 2009.
ANDREW STRONGITHARM

Left: Looking south at Imberhorne Lane Bridge in October 2009. STEPHEN FAIRWEATHER

Bluebell centenarian president Bernard Holden (left) watches the waste by road operation on 25 November 2008.

Waste by road

Mayor of East Grinstead, Councillor Ginnie Waddingham at the controls of the excavator, loading the first bucketful of spoil.

From Bluebell News Winter 2008.

For some months now, focus has been on getting the project manoeuvred into a position whereby a start could be made on removing some of the waste in Imberhorne Cutting. That the first lorry load of waste left site on Tuesday 25 November 2008 in front of the mayor of East Grinstead, local councillors and invited guests, is now history. Suffice to say that even the weather was kind and the publicity well received. It was something of a landmark day for the project and the culmination of several years of hard work getting to the point where we actually could remove the spoil.

The months leading up to this pilot phase have been hectic and, like most of the project, pretty challenging in terms of getting all of the requirements in place – and getting enough money to carry out the work. The aim was to remove sufficient volumes of Municipal Solid Waste (MSW) so that we could more accurately predict the removal costs, timescales, methodology and, crucially, find out the true cutting profile – as this was believed to have been altered during the original infilling process.

Having identified Land & Water as our partner we then had to agree the form of contract. In common with many civil engineering works these days, increasing use is made of a form of contract entitled 'NEC3 Engineering and Construction Contract' which is very much based on the principle of early contractor involvement with the client. This route has many advantages; not least the reduced tendering timescales and costs, which ultimately the client pays for one way or another.

Instead, both parties meet and agree how the work should be done, how it will be costed, what the margins are, what the risks are and who carries them – from which a target cost is agreed. If the work costs less, the savings are shared and if it costs more then this too is shared. The whole principle is one

Temporary roadways have been laid on top of the tip to enable lorries to enter the wheel cleaning area and on to the public highway.

of an open book partnership approach, based on sharing the pain or gain resulting from the works. This is well suited to Bluebell's requirements because it keeps costs down and allows our active participation.

October saw the construction of the site compound at Imberhorne Lane get underway, the site straddles our own land adjacent to the cutting and also land owned by Mid Sussex District Council who granted us a lease for its portion to cover the duration of the works with access via the Civic Amenity Site in Imberhorne Lane. The site layout, having been carefully designed on a merry-go-round principle is complete with offices, messing facilities, toilets, storage and parking and was then marked out ready for construction.

Roads, fencing, services and gates were all carried out under the supervision of infrastructure manager Matt Crawford and volunteer gangs led by Nigel Longdon and Ian Aitken.

Land & Water then began preparatory works involving such things as construction of the leachate capture facilities, dust monitors, odour monitors, safety systems, exposure of Hill Place Farm Bridge ready for inspection and laying down the temporary haul roads on top of the tip surface.

In parallel with all of this work our lawyers and insurers had to make sure we complied with the requirements of the sale contract for the cutting from West Sussex County Council, which was more challenging than expected.

Since the start of removal, a typical day sees around 35 lorries leaving site with an average load of 19.5 tons of, so far, fairly dry MSW. As predicted the long reach digger can load lorries quicker than there are lorries available to be loaded. We could utilise more but it would be mighty expensive to have them standing around waiting if anything goes wrong, so we need a balancing act. The contents are much as expected – mostly household waste plus old washing machines, tyres, rubble and bits of metal. We have exposed the cutting embankments, exposed the bridge and found the old trackbed.

Some early data from the trial suggests that we are clearing around 10 metres of the cutting each week at a current cost of £110,00 per week based on 35 lorries a day each carrying just under 20 tons, which means there is some 3250 tons in each 10 metre slice of infill. With 355 metres of the cutting left it will therefore take a further 33.5 weeks to finish the job; moving around 109,000 tons of MSW at a cost of £3.685m which roughly equates to the original estimate of £4m to do the whole job.

Chris White.

Scooping spoil at the north end of the cutting adjacent to Hill Place Farm Bridge.
ALL: BRIAN SHARPE

Waste by Rail

by Chris White

From Bluebell News Autumn 2009.

Turning to progress with removal of the waste from Imberhorne Cutting, I hinted in the last *Bluebell News* that we might have found a more cost-effective option for getting rid of this stuff. I can now confirm we have negotiated a package to do just that. Following lengthy discussions with Network Rail and the rail freight sector, rail rather than road transport is now once again possible. This was always the preferred method but was met with numerous obstacles when we originally tried to adopt this approach. However, the climate is now such that pathways and trains are available and we can make this happen with a significant overall cost reduction.

Next spring, probably in March, the first train load of infill will leave the north end of Imberhorne Cutting, carrying 1000 tons of waste bound for a rail connected waste site at Calvert in Buckinghamshire. The train will be provided by GBRf (part of the First Group), the waste will be loaded at Imberhorne Cutting by Land & Water and then handled and dumped at the destination by Shanks. The joint research we have undertaken with industry suggests it is possible to handle one train load per day and we will trial this over a five-day period to see how successful the operation is. Effectively one train will dispose of the same amount as 50 lorry loads did during the road based trial earlier this year. The carbon footprint advantage in using rail speaks for itself but I will provide more specific comparison details in a future report.

Cost-wise the savings are attractive. If this trial works as we think it should, the cost of moving the remaining material will be around £2.9 million, a saving of £0.7m against the predicted road movement based on today's prices and what we know about the volumes remaining. Obviously the prices are not fixed and can change over time depending on how long it takes to complete the removal works. The volumes and density could also change as we dig further into the mass but this is a good indication of what is possible.

However, one of the great attractions of this method of working is the significant reduction of mobilisation and demobilisations costs compared with road. The need for extensive site facilities at Imberhorne, including a costly wheel wash, are

This view looking south shows the different levels that have been 'carved' to effectively load spoil into wagons. **PHIL BARNES**

Not a canal restoration. The exposed bridge at Hill Place Farm and the result of the Waste by Road operation.

reduced to simple messing and storage that can be provided at minimal cost by us rather than the contractor. Plant can be hired in and out as required so future clearance work can be undertaken in much smaller chunks as money becomes available rather than having to wait until larger sums are in the bank to justify the mobilisation costs. Both GBRf and Shanks have indicated they can respond to our funding availability quite quickly so we could 'switch' the process 'on and off' in a far more responsive low-cost way than with road. Clear progress would therefore be demonstrated with the two railheads getting closer as each chunk of waste is removed, which in turn will hopefully encourage people to dig into their pockets to help 'close the gap'.

CHRIS WHITE

From Bluebell News Summer 2010.
Now for news of the pilot trial of 'Waste by Rail', as it has become known. Tuesday 6 July will see the first official train leave East Grinstead loaded with around 1000 tons of waste from Imberhorne Cutting bound for a Shanks landfill site on the Bedford branch of the West Coast Main Line. Made up of 18 wagons these trains will be operated by GBRf (now owned by Eurotunnel) and will be hauled by a Class 66 diesel locomotive.

Because of weight restrictions on the line between East Grinstead and South Croydon, special dispensation has been granted by Network Rail for these trains to operate. However, one of the conditions is that each wagon has a weight limit imposed, which means we have to verify the contents of each wagon before it leaves site. To do this a modern form of weighbridge is being installed. This device, which is fixed to the rails, weighs each axle electronically from which the overall wagon weight is calculated.

In order to manage the train movements on site and to liaise with the Oxted signaller, a team of specially trained Bluebell 'operators' is required to ensure the safe operation of the train while on Bluebell metals and also to protect people working on site while train movements are taking place. The majority of these are drawn from the ever-willing pool of volunteers involved in the project with the necessary written procedure and assessment processes being produced with the help of the railway's operations manager. This aspect is probably something readers will not have thought about but is one of several behind the scenes activities necessary before the trial can happen.

Naturally there is going to be a great deal of interest in these trains from both members and the public alike. Because space on site is so limited – especially now that the permanent way is in place – access will have to be fairly strictly controlled. There will be a public and press launch on the evening of Tuesday 6 July 2010 with some limited space being available for members and public which will be subject to an entry fee at the gate. Because the 'Waste by Rail' pilot is now so close to the planned original official opening of the station scheduled for 3 July, this is now going to be re-scheduled to coincide with the commencement of the first shuttle trains

In case one should think that work stops on the extension in bad weather, these were the dire conditions of 17 December 2010. PAT PLANE

Wagon loading at the 'quarry face' on 3 December 2011. ANDREW STRONGITHARM

Looking south from Hill Place Farm Bridge on 29 November 2011. The diggers in the centre distance are bringing waste down to the railhead. STEPHEN FAIRWEATHER

operating in September. This will enable a much more high profile event to be organised – with the added benefit of allowing us more time to deal with those delayed edging slabs referred to earlier and putting the final finishing touches to the site.

Once the 'Waste by Rail' pilot is completed, the results can be analysed in both financial and logistical terms. We can then assess how much can be moved next, hopefully later this year. Assuming the pilot is successful and subject to funding, we would like to undertake a four-week run in October, which would really make a difference.

From Bluebell News Spring 2011.
'WASTE BY RAIL 2' GOES TO PLAN
We are into week two of 'WBR2' and progress is much as expected. Naturally there have been teething problems but these are not significant enough to warrant space here; overall there have been no 'show-stoppers' to worry about. The small group of Bluebell volunteers and contractors working on site each day have gelled into an efficient team with the common aim of maximising the potential for removing muck as efficiently as possible. The days themselves are long and so far the weather has been less than friendly most of the time – but that's no more than was expected.

There has however been one surprise – with the discovery of a massive cache of old tyres laying quite deep at the north end. These have to be removed and stacked elsewhere on the site for future processing as they cannot go to landfill. This takes time and impacts on accessing the waste for loading but on the plus side it is less volume that has to be loaded into wagons, and every little helps. While some tyres have been encountered previously and more were expected, nothing quite as big as this was on the cards.

Currently the excavators are working under power lines that cross the north end of the site, which means for the long reach machine in particular, great care is required and this tends to slow progress. From time to time the coloured bunting which warns the drivers of their proximity to these power lines gets damaged and these have to be quickly repaired, a very muddy and tricky job. Once clear of this area the excavators will be able to work unhindered as they progress southwards.

The trains themselves and the GBRf crews that

Saturday 19 November 2011 after the first week of WBR5. This shows quite a transformation at the southern end of the tip at Imberhorne Lane. STEPHEN FAIRWEATHER

man them are excellent; arriving and departing on, or very near, booked time and doing the job intended very efficiently. The shunter in particular is on the go the whole time as each train is loaded in two wagon sets, which means a lot of coupling and uncoupling. He says he's lost weight but got fitter! As progress is made into the cutting and more track panels laid, so the number of wagons loaded in each set will increase and his running around will reduce.

The make-up of the waste itself is proving to be of interest, of the 7000 (approx) tons moved so far, the proportion of soil, concrete and metal is quite high. The concrete can be crushed and reused and the metal sold but the high soil content is leading us to investigate the viability of screening the waste to remove recyclable 'soil' that need not go to landfill. Obviously this will become a straightforward financial assessment based on which is the cheaper option, pay to remove as it is against the cost of screening it to reduce the volumes transported away.

Guidance on what we can and cannot do with the waste generally is provided by the Environment Agency with whom we have worked closely throughout the project. They are very supportive of our aims, come on site regularly to discuss progress and offer direction on how to maximise the operation while dealing with the tip in a responsible way. The results of the project are also being fed into their case study files to provide others with guidance on best practice in the clearance of railway cuttings, apparently this is a quite widespread issue in the UK. This is probably a heritage railway 'first' in true Bluebell fashion and it's good to think our pioneering spirit is alive and well but also implies we cannot afford to fail.

Overall then, this report has a positive spin about it so doubtless readers will conclude all is going to plan and so enquire what happens next? Well WBR3, 4, 5 and so on is the order of the day until we have removed sufficient waste to get the two rail-heads connected. Certainly the majority of the waste by rail component must be completed by April 2012 to avoid paying Landfill Tax – but as always this goal is dependant on funding being available. A further consideration that is crucial to WBR is train pathway availability and already we are having to reserve slots through to next March in order to run these trains and once firmed up, funding has to be in place to match them or the pathways be released with the consequential high risk of not securing enough to do the job in time, a sobering thought for readers to ponder.

CHRIS WHITE

The last two wagons of the day being loaded on 22 November 2011. STEPHEN FAIRWEATHER

From Bluebell News Summer 2011.
I start by reflecting on the overall progress that has been made since acquisition of the key plot of land north of Kingscote in 2002, which enabled us to start laying track towards Imberhorne Lane and what that landmark event did to trigger a restart of the project. Looking at the milestones achieved since then tends to put things into perspective and actually makes clearance of the remaining filled cutting seem a relatively routine task, albeit an expensive one.

In summary we have:
• Made good the formation from Kingscote to Imberhorne Lane and constructed a railway along this section.
• Cleared the spoil from both sides of Imberhorne Lane Bridge.
• Undertaken a 'Waste By Road' pilot, removing 10,000 tons of waste.
• Constructed a platform and trackwork at East Grinstead.
• Commissioned a connection with the national network at East Grinstead.
• Waterproofed and laid track across the viaduct southwards to the cutting.
• Undertaken a 'Waste By Rail' pilot, removing 4600 tons of waste.
• Refined the 'Waste By Rail' process and removed a further 17,780 tons in 2011.
• Negotiated with stakeholders and dealt with legislative issues that combined probably took as many man hours as all the above put together.

All in all quite an achievement, which would not have been possible without the massive volunteer resource input over the years. Turning now to this year's WBR2, which seems to have been watched by everyone and commented on by many, it's worth setting down the official view of this phase. In essence 'Waste By Rail' is a winning formula and WBR2 in particular worked well; the whole process is probably refined to a point that is as good as it gets and will form the

Rubbish: The cleared area seen from the centre of the cutting at the end of WBR5, November 2011. CHRIS WHITE

An East Grinstead station open day in September 2011 allowed members of the public to ride over the viaduct and down to the tip courtesy of the railway's 4-Vep unit being propelled by a Class 73 locomotive. ANDREW STRONGITHARM

With the lighting tower necessary for late afternoon working, four items of plant go about their business while they await the next wagonload on 2 December 2011. ANDREW STRONGITHARM

core approach to removal of the remaining waste. The cost to excavate, transport and dump is £25 per ton, with each train carrying around 900 tons in 18 wagons; future trains are expected to consist of 20 wagons, increasing the load to around 980 tons. Like most things, if you plan, plan and plan again, going over all the component parts, then there is every chance it will work for real; and that is exactly what happened with WBR2.

What next?

WBR is set to continue with 20-wagon trains, and around 60 more of these are required between now and April 2012 to remove sufficient waste to join up the two railheads at either end of the cutting before Landfill Tax kicks in. In detail these trains are broken down into the following stages:

• WBR3. Three weeks commencing 4 July (14,800 tons).
• WBR4. Two weeks commencing 15 August (9850 tons).
• WBR5. Three weeks commencing 26 September (13,800 tons).
• WBR6. Four weeks in 2012 (20,746 tons, dates yet to be confirmed).

To some extent the dates for WBR3-5 are dictated by available train paths and wagon availability, but factors such as Bluebell's resources and funding streams also play a part in deciding what can be done and when. WBR6 is the last and longest phase before next April, and so far funding is not yet in place for this crucial four-week stint.

The current cost projection to move the estimated 59,196 tons comprising WBR3–6 is £1.483 million, with another £0.5m for track and signalling – which equates to the £2m generally quoted as the cost to connect the two railheads.

What does this mean?

• Around 60–70% of the waste will have been removed from the cutting before Landfill Tax has to be paid, and it will be possible to join up the two railheads during 2012.
• It gives us time to assess how to deal with the residual waste, in the meantime sending out a strong message saying that we've done it, there's a railway from Sheffield Park to East Grinstead, with a main line connection.

• Completion of signalling and legislative formalities to enable public passenger trains to run can take place during 2012.

On the subject of track and signalling, it's probably worth laying to rest speculation surrounding these subjects. Firstly signalling. The solution remains in that a two-stage approach is being adopted. The first consists of alterations at Kingscote to control the single line to East Grinstead, with the ground frames remaining in situ. The second, at some time in the future, will abolish the ground frames and introduce remote control of the points and signalling from Kingscote. Both have to be minimal cost 'fit for purpose' solutions that do not involve construction of a signal box at East Grinstead. There are much greater demands for S&T expertise elsewhere on the railway. There are no plans to retain the loading siding at Imberhorne North.

From Bluebell News, Winter 2011.
As WBR5 concludes, some 75,000 tons of waste will have been removed from Imberhorne cutting. It is possible one more phase may be required in early 2012 to complete the extraction process, but that will not be confirmed until we have finished the next stage of design work. We had to get to where we are now before this could be undertaken with any certainty. Having said that I get the feeling from talking to the site team they are almost disappointed at the prospect of no more waste trains to look after!

At this point it's worth summarising where we are with this aspect of the project, so here are some key facts:

1) We are at the concluding stage of agreeing a 'Deed of Variation' with West Sussex County Council (WSCC) to change the terms under which we originally purchased the cutting. The principle is that only sufficient waste will be removed to enable us to reinstate the railway. As you might imagine there are various other conditions such as how we make good the residual waste and manage any future contamination risks. These negotiations have been going on since February with the full support of WSCC, who

The view north from Imberhorne Lane on 19 February 2012, exposing the same rock formation seen in the 1957 photo opposite. STEPHEN FAIRWEATHER

acknowledge our motives but understandably are keen to ensure that the council is free of liability should the railway close down at some time in the future.

2) This change in strategy is possible because the waste has proved to be more stable than expected, contains very little leachate and has a high solids content, while the cutting itself contains much more clay and soil than any of the originals surveys indicated.

3) However, because we are leaving some residual waste there is an impact on other stakeholders such as our insurers, Mid Sussex District Council and the Environment Agency, and all of these have to be consulted. Agreement needs to be reached on how we proceed and, crucially, how we mitigate any risk to neighbours and watercourses.

4) The final cutting shape will change as a result of leaving residual waste, so our engineering designs – which were based on original data derived from a consultant's report undertaken in the 1980s – must also change. The data indicated that the cutting was filled with domestic waste and capped off as it stood on closure of the railway. In reality the western cutting face and both cutting shoulders were further excavated, presumably to make room for additional material or possibly to use the sandstone for other purposes. The cutting no longer has anything like a conventional profile. This only came to light after excavation commenced.

5) Our revised design must therefore take into account both the emerging shape of the cutting and the waste which will remain in it. One of the reasons for shifting the excavation route from the western to the eastern side is the integrity of the sandstone face, which is less damaged and so far has presented a profile that does not require any

This aerial view gives a clearer picture as to what is going on on the ground, with three diggers in operation the temporary 'bridge' can be seen, allowing access to the two 'halves' of the cutting, taken on 14 September 2012. **PHILIP LANE PHOTOGRAPHY**

remedial work. This in turn suggests we made the right decision.

6) Appearances can be deceptive, so do not assume that because there still seems to be a lot of waste blocking the cutting that there is a lot more to remove from site. The unexpected shape of the cutting and waste composition works to our advantage, in that it enables some re-engineering of the residual waste to take place and so further reduce what goes to landfill. In short the design team is quite satisfied with the position it finds itself in, and is developing a number of options to finalise the formation shape ready for constructing the railway itself. A series of pictures showing the cutting surface on completion of WBR5 is included to illustrate just what has been achieved. Remember 75,000 tons of waste have been removed, and it shows.

7) What does distort the picture on site is the vast amount of capping material which has deliberately been stored for the time being, rather than diverting vital funds away from WBR activities to clear it away. Once this material is removed however, and the cutting re-profiled, things will take on a more traditional railway feel.

Finally on this subject, some tidying up and general work will continue on site for a while. Then operations will close down until next year when the weather and daylight hours will be more conducive to what we are doing.

For most of 2012 the emphasis will be on completing work at East Grinstead, along with constructing the railway through the cutting itself and clearing away the capping material.

CHRIS WHITE

C2X No 32440 heads the 12.28pm ex-East Grinstead through Imberhorne Cutting on 21 March 1957. COLIN HOGG

Bluebell spoil trains to Bedfordshire

The Summer 2011 edition of *Bluebell News* contained a letter from Derek Thorogood and a reply from Chris White about the running of Bluebell Railway spoil trains on WBR1-3. Member Peter Underwood, an employee of South West Trains, with assistance from industry colleagues Peter Starks and Paul Taylor, gives more detail.

The GBRf trains are normally formed of a Class 66 locomotive with MLA wagons which can travel up to 60mph and are worked by Train Managers (drivers) from Ferme Park, Tonbridge and Willesden depots, and ATM's (assistant train managers) who carry out shunting duties at Forder's Sidings, Bedford and East Grinstead. Upon arrival at Forder's Sidings the train is shunted into a siding that can accommodate the entire train and then the wagons are unloaded by a digger directly onto the landfill site.

Depending on exam requirements, the same locomotives may work the train between one to five days each week, although normally the same loco is deployed all week and fuelled at Forder's every other morning. Where possible, the same train managers work the same turns for most of the week, but do change around. This is not only for rostering purposes but retention of route knowledge at that depot.

The original train formation was 18 MLA wagons, but for the most recent batch of trains, this was increased to 19 wagons and it is planned to extend to 20 wagons in future. Experience in operating the train meant the additional wagons could be added to increase the efficiency of how much tonnage can be moved on each train.

The loading procedure at East Grinstead is quite complex, with the train being run-round in two halves at the Bluebell station and three wagons being split off, loaded and weighed at the 'tip face' at a time. The train crew, loaders and Bluebell staff on site are fully employed with loading activities during the afternoon.

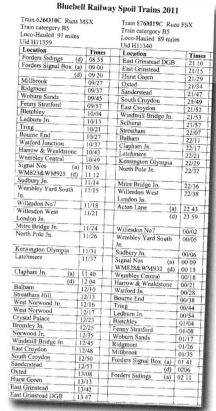

Bluebell Railway Spoil Trains 2011

Train 626O10C Runs MSX — Train catergory B5 — Loco-Hauled 91 miles — Uid H11359

Location		Times
Forders Sidings	(d)	08 55
Forders Signal Box	(a)	09 00
	(d)	09 20
Millbrook		09/27
Ridgmont		09/37
Woburn Sands		09/45
Fenny Stratford		09/57
Bletchley		10/04
Ledburn Jn.		10/13
Tring		10/21
Bourne End		10/27
Watford Junction		10/37
Harrow & Wealdstone		10/43
Wembley Central		10/49
Signal Nos	(a)	10 56
WM823&WM925	(d)	11 12
Sudbury Jn.		11/14
Wembley Yard South Jn.		11/15
Willesden No7		11/18
Willesden West London Jn.		11/21
Mitre Bridge Jn.		11/24
North Pole Jn.		11/26
Kensington Olympia		11/31
Latchmere		11/37
Clapham Jn.	(a)	11 40
	(d)	12 04
Balham		12/10
Streatham Hill		12/13
West Norwood Jn.		12/16
West Norwood		12/17
Crystal Palace		12/23
Bromley Jn.		12/25
Norwood Jn.		12/35
Windmill Bridge Jn.		12/45
East Croydon		12/48
South Croydon		12/50
Sanderstead		12/53
Oxted		13/08
Hurst Green		13/13
East Grinstead		13/42
East Grinstead DGB		13 47

Train 876M19C Runs FSX — Train catergory B5 — Loco-Hauled 89 miles — Uid H11340

Location		Times
East Grinstead DGB		21 10
East Grinstead		21/15
Hurst Green		21/29
Oxted		21/34
Sanderstead		21/49
South Croydon		21/49
East Croydon		21/52
Windmill Bridge Jn.		21/53
Selhurst		21/57
Streatham		22/07
Balham		22/11
Clapham Jn.		22/17
Latchmere		22/21
Kensington Olympia		22/29
North Pole Jn.		22/32
Mitre Bridge Jn.		22/36
Willesden West London Jn.		22/38
Acton Lane	(a)	22 43
	(d)	23 59
Willesden No7		00/02
Wembley Yard South Jn.		00/05
Sudbury Jn.		00/06
Signal Nos	(a)	00 09
WM828&WM932	(d)	00 15
Wembley Central		00/18
Harrow & Wealdstone		00/21
Watford Jn.		00/28
Bourne End		00/38
Tring		00/44
Ledburn Jn.		00/54
Bletchley		01/04
Fenny Stratford		01/08
Woburn Sands		01/17
Ridgmont		01/26
Millbrook		01/35
Forders Signal Box	(a)	0206
	(d)	
Forders Sidings	(a)	02 11

A typical timetable and (below) train consist and outlined drivers diagrams. This information was gathered by Peter Underwood during WBR3 which ran from 4-22 July 2011.

No 66707 has reversed its empty wagons from Forder's Sidings onto the Down line of the Marston Vale line on 18 July before heading west towards Bletchley.

No 66707 heads empty wagons through Stewartby station towards Bletchley for London and East Grinstead.

No 66473 backs its empty wagons out of Forder's Sidings on 14 July. ALL: RICHARD CRANE

Consist of Empty Train 6O10 08 55 Forder's Sidings to East Grinstead DGB

Locomotive
66707 GBCM

Wagons
503075 E MLA BLUEBELL, 503003 E MLA BLUEBELL, 503059 E MLA BLUEBELL
503010 E MLA BLUEBELL, 503002 E MLA BLUEBELL, 503005 E MLA BLUEBELL
503038 E MLA BLUEBELL, 503004 E MLA BLUEBELL, 503035 E MLA BLUEBELL
503049 E MLA BLUEBELL, 503074 E MLA BLUEBELL, 503073 E MLA BLUEBELL
503041 E MLA BLUEBELL, 503032 E MLA BLUEBELL, 503013 E MLA BLUEBELL
503039 E MLA BLUEBELL, 503036 E MLA BLUEBELL, 503024 E MLA BLUEBELL
503045 E MLA BLUEBELL

0 LDS 19 MTYS 475 TONNES 1064FT/324MTR 400 POTENTIAL AIR BRAKE FORCE

1 UNITS 3300 HORSEPOWER 127 TONS 70FT/21MTR 68 BRAKE FORCE.

Drivers Diagrams

Willesden Diagram
Works train from 0855 to 1056
Tonbridge Diagram
Works train from 1056 to 1615

Tonbridge Diagram
Works train from 1615 to 2243
Ferme Park or Willesden Diagram
Works train from 2359 to 0211

Assistant Train Managers are at Forder's Sidings and East Grinstead to carry out shunting duties.

Member Richard Crane of Bedford describes 'the other end of the journey'.
The landfill site at Forder's Sidings were formerly part of one of the largest brickworks in the country at Stewartby. Production at the works contracted over the past 20 years or so and a large part of the site was developed for landfill by Shanks & McEwan. The majority of the rubbish brought to the site came by container trains from Cricklewood, north London, over a period of nearly 26 years. The trains finished three years ago when the site was declared 'full'. It was therefore of great interest when locally we heard that the Bluebell's rubbish was coming to Bedfordshire. The cap on the landfill site was removed in part and Bluebell's rubbish was almost certainly to be the last before the site is finally capped and sealed. There are no other rail activities at Forder's Sidings at present, although a number of sidings remain in situ.

The photos show the train of empty wagons shunted out of Forder's Sidings towards Bedford on the Marston Vale branch line from Bletchley and then heading towards Bletchley and on to East Grinstead through Stewartby station.

The parapet is all that is visible of the bridge in 2003 following the creation of the landfill site in the 1960s by East Grinstead Town Council. MIKE ESAU

Hill Place Farm Bridge looking north at the East Grinstead distant signal on 2 May 1968. PAUL LEAVENS

Then & Now: Hill Place Farm Bridge

Below: Looking north at Hill Place the evening before the opening day to public traffic, Friday 22 March 2013. COLIN TYSON

Three views from approximately the same location looking north towards Hill Place Farm Bridge (notice the tree line) – vegetation being cleared from the top of the tip on 9 February 2008; the scene on 21 March 2009 – the mounds being part of the clay capping which had been moved after the trial of waste by road; 19 March 2011 and the area has been transformed after five weeks of waste removal by rail. Between the first and third view, about 31,750 tonnes of waste has been removed. STEPHEN FAIRWEATHER

Works at Hill Pl[a

An engineers' possession of Hill Place Farm Bridge, the occupation bridge situated at the northern end of Imberhorne Cutting, during the late summer of 2010, enabled much-needed repair work to be undertaken by contractors to West Sussex County Council (WSCC).

Repairs to make the now-exposed bridge safe on the underside, following dislodging of the brick rings which give the bridge its strength (probably by the machinery used to deposit the original waste), are being funded by owners WSCC, which also own Imberhorne Lane Bridge.

The north face (East Grinstead side) of Hill Place Farm Bridge during the erection of the very extensive scaffolding.

The north face, with the scaffolding and safety netting in place, after volunteers had removed most of the vegetation, mainly ivy. The south face of this bridge had much less vegetation, which was removed prior to the start of the tip removal.

The south (tip) side of the bridge.

e Farm Bridge

The start of remedial work on the southern arch. ALL: STEPHEN FAIRWEATHER

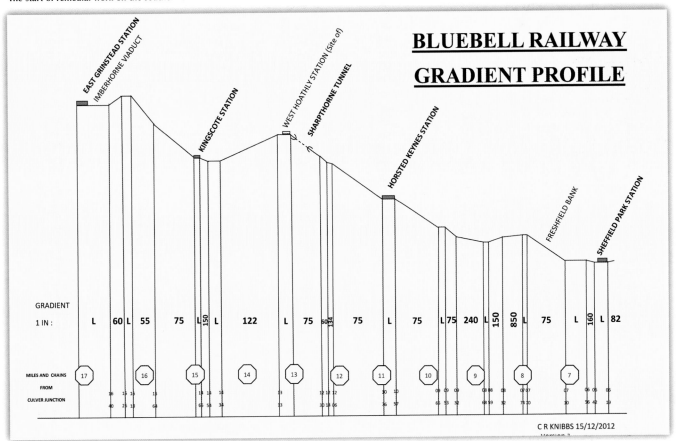

Up until the last completed section from Kingscote to East Grinstead, the summit of the line was at the foot crossing at the site of the former station at West Hoathly. With the gradient being banked further at the tip edges to reduce the amount of spoil removed, the summit is now within the cutting and has been labelled 'Holden Summit'. This is the latest version of the gradient diagram, created by operations manager Chris Knibbs.

Bringing in the ballast

No 66721 *Harry Beck* and its wagons unload new washed and graded second-hand ballast on 30 October 2010, in preparation for laying the siding north of Imberhorne. STEPHEN FAIRWEATHER

Wednesday 28 November 2012 was quite historic, as it was the first time a main line locomotive had ventured along the newly laid track (with a ballast train) and the railway has not had wagons this far into the cutting before either. STEPHEN FAIRWEATHER

Ballast and track being manually worked north of Imberhorne Lane on 5 March 2013. ANDREW STRONGITHARM

Loading ballast in Imberhorne Cutting for transfer south on 28 March 2013. GRAHAM MALLINSON

Completing the Northern Extension Project

The penultimate ballast train before completion of the extension is seen unloading at Hill Place on 21 February. JON BOWERS

Laying of a track panel in Imberhorne Cutting on 4 March 2013. GRAHAM MALLINSON

Well we did it on time as planned. In fact, rather than much rushing round on the Friday before opening, it was a relatively relaxed day focusing on the usual last minute tidying up tasks. As for all the hype and media attention, this is well reported elsewhere so I do not propose to comment further – except to say we've certainly been the focus of great interest from wide ranging groups, some of which has not necessarily been desirable during test and gauging runs.

And so the extension was finally handed over to the operators on Friday 22 March following completion of Safety Verification which had taken up quite a bit of time during the previous few days. This process now resides entirely 'in house' under current legislation. However, because of the rather unusual nature of this project we have worked closely with the Railway Inspectorate to make sure our engineering approach was acceptable and there would be no show stoppers come Entry Into Service. Consequently a joint walk-over was held prior to Safety Verification so we could present the finished product and deal with any questions the inspector may wish to be answered. As history now shows, this exercise went well and following a check of our Safety Verification file, he saw no reason to prevent us proceeding with EIS on 23 March. It's always a good idea to remember that railway inspectors have enormous powers and consultation is much better than enforcement, as some railways have discovered over time.

In terms of progress up to the deadline, Nemesis continued to plague the project to the very end, not the weather this time but in the form of tamper problems. Having arrived later than booked it required repairs before use and then suffered further problems which resulted in delays to test trains and crew training, which all had to be compressed into a week. The two deliveries of ballast, some 2,000 tons in total, quickly got consumed as the tamper lifted and lined the track putting up to two inches of cant on in places. We now await a further 1,000-ton delivery to top up and give a final tamp to deal with settlement which will inevitably occur during the heavy two weeks of festival traffic. When completed this should leave the Kingscote to East Grinstead section in a good state for the future.

So what next? There is still a list of jobs to close out over the coming weeks, many

Left: Connection of railheads immediately south of Imberhorne Lane bridge (approx 4pm on 7 March 2013), and pulling sleepers underneath rails, prior to the gauging run of light Class 66 diesel from Tonbridge Yard to Sheffield Park and return a few hours later. It also gives a sense of the scale of plant involved at the end game. GRAHAM MALLINSON

The first 'train' to pass over the completed extension (as opposed to P.Way trolley, road-railer, tamper or light Class 66 diesel) from Sheffield Park to East Grinstead was the 11.39 ex-SP ECS on 9 March of 'on-hire' Crompton No 33103 *Swordfish*, seen approaching Imberhorne Cutting having picked up the Mk. 1 coach for East Grinstead buffet, and a brake van. GRAHAM MALLINSON

The first steam working through to East Grinstead was the 1.40pm 'training test train' with 9F 2-10-0 No 92212 on 16 March, seen approaching Imberhorne Lane. GRAHAM MALLINSON

of these are of a minor nature but significantly completing earthworks in the cutting and yet more drainage remain the dominant civil engineering tasks while construction of the ticket office canopy has to be fitted in as well. As things stand we plan to close out the project at the end of April and then move on to other jobs around the railway. However, this target is largely influenced by available funds and the ever-challenging weather. What we are keen to avoid is completion works dragging on for months.

Talking of other jobs, the NEP team, which has grown from strength to strength over the past couple of years or so, is a valuable resource that has proved itself time after time. We are therefore keen to retain this expertise for other infrastructure projects both large and small, for the extension would not have happened without them.

Also gratifying, has been the incredible flow of congratulatory messages from both within the railway and outside. We have been admired for our professional approach to the project by several key stakeholders, including Network Rail. The bond which developed between contractors and ourselves during construction dates back several years now and is undoubtedly a proven exemplar of how to achieve a common goal. This I believe is a major factor in the project's success and my own thanks must go to everyone involved for the incredible support and belief I have been entrusted with, for this alone the only option was onwards and upwards.

Lastly, more about what we have planned for the future in the next issue and some prioritisation is required before going public on our workload. We also need to get to grips with the final NEP activities. Future reports will therefore continue but with a more general theme that hopefully keeps you informed about what's going on in 'Infrastructure' once NEP is no more.

CHRIS WHITE
Infrastructure director

At a low-key 'Golden Spike' ceremony for NEP workers on 8 March, Northern Extension team 'Mum' Barbara Watkins tightens the bolts on the 'White Fishplate' under Imberhorne Lane Bridge. After the 'ceremony', rails were removed and 60ft lengths put back in their place. GRAHAM MALLINSON

NEP working volunteers were given the chance to ride in the first steam 'test train' working to East Grinstead on 16 March. Chris White drove the 9F, stopping on the second run for this photograph just on the north side of Hill Place Bridge. MICHAEL HOPPS

Hill Place Bridge to Imberhorne Viaduct

Above: Looking north towards East Grinstead from Hill Place Farm Bridge on 5 December 2008 with evidence of trackbed clearance and engineers' surveying. ANDREW STRONGITHARM

Above right: The tranquil view south of the viaduct on 14 November 2009. This is one of the few Bluebell locations that amazingly retains its lineside fencing that dates from the construction of the line. STEPHEN FAIRWEATHER

Right: Ballasting reaches the new railhead at the newly-refurbished Hill Place Farm Bridge in November 2010. PAT PLANE

Just round the curve from the photo above (right) is the exposed bridge at Hill Place with the filled in cutting beyond still evident in January 2009. ANDREW STRONGITHARM

Nine empty wagons are being pushed towards the tip by No 66720 *Metronet Pathfinder* on 26 February 2011. STEPHEN FAIRWEATHER

Looking north from Hill Place Farm Bridge on 25 February 2011 with four spoil wagons filled and track panels (left), for extending into the cutting. STEPHEN FAIRWEATHER

The 'Mine of Serpents' railtour arrived at East Grinstead and proceeded down to the railhead at Imberhorne Cutting on 5 November 2011, consisting of 10 coaches, top and tailed by Nos 73141 *Charlotte* and 73208 *Kirsten*. STEPHEN FAIRWEATHER

Left: A 'wagon holding' siding was built at this location during the construction period and removed prior to Entry Into Service. To the right is the temporary weigh house, which checked wagon axle loads prior to them returning to the main line and onwards to the waste disposal point. ANDREW STRONGITHARM

Hill Place Viaduct

Until the Northern Extension Project was first mooted, the most impressive civil engineering structure on the five-mile Bluebell Railway between Sheffield Park and Horsted Keynes was Three Arch Bridge (sometimes referred to as Nobles Bridge) – an occupation overbridge of red brick situated in a cutting just south of Horsted Keynes.

Aside from Sharpthorne Tunnel, the most visually impressive civil engineering structure on the extended line has to be the 10-arch Hill Place Viaduct (also known as Imberhorne Viaduct), which makes for a triumphal entry into East Grinstead from the south and traverses a valley that is still rural at its south end and built up with residential streets at its north end.

Construction started in 1879. Built of red brick, the viaduct is 262 yards long and was Grade II Listed by English Heritage on 15 September 1988, as 'an imposing and unaltered structure'.

At its highest point above ground – at the fifth arch from the East Grinstead end – it crosses a small stream called the Ouse, which at one point is 93ft below the crown of the arch. The stream a mile or so further on flows into the infant River Medway, which the line itself crosses near Kingscote.

The viaduct came into Bluebell Railway ownership from British Rail in September 1992 for the obligatory £1. Initial repairs to arches and parapets were undertaken at a cost of £175,000, which was largely met from Landfill Tax Credits awards. Volunteers then took over for laying a waterproof membrane on the deck, repointing and graffiti removal and running a drainage network that collects rainwater and distributes it to a holding tank for pumping to the (currently under construction) locomotive water tower at East Grinstead station.

Hill Place Viaduct, looking to the west, on 23 December 1985. MIKE ESAU

Contractors working on the Viaduct parapets. TONY SULLIVAN

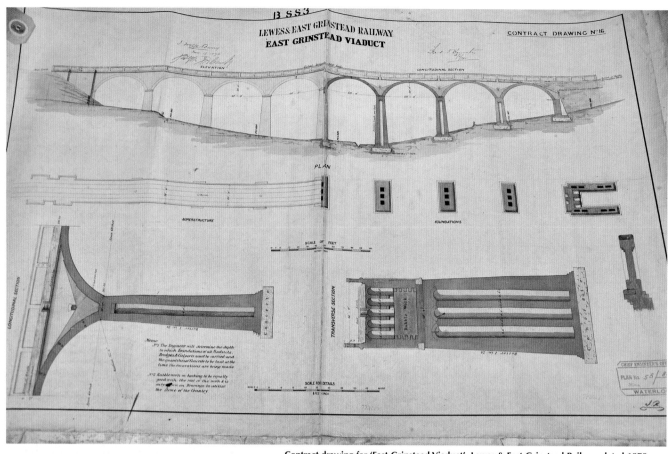

Contract drawing for 'East Grinstead Viaduct', Lewes & East Grinstead Railway, dated 1878, the year before construction started. BLUEBELL ARCHIVE

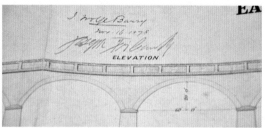

The above drawing is hand signed by both Joseph Firbank and J Wolfe Barry – Barry being the consulting engineer to the promoters of the line and a pupil of Henry Brunel, son of the great Isambard. London's Tower Bridge was to be Barry's most well-known achievement.

Bluebell News winter 2009: Waterproofing of the viaduct surface is complete and all the drainage and service ducts have been installed. Sleepers and rail are being rolled out ready to extend the track across the viaduct and just beyond to the cattle creep. Nigel Longdon and his team will now begin the laborious but all important task of securing the edge of the waterproof membrane to both sides of the viaduct wall then finishing it off with a cement filler to provide a weatherproof and smart look.

It has been interesting to watch the viaduct appearance gradually change from a neglected structure to a functional one again as work has progressed over the past year. The final touch will, of course, be the presence of a railway line once again. Overall the project is a credit to Matt Crawford and his team who have worked through all weathers to achieve an impressive and highly professional result.

CHRIS WHITE

Viaduct enters Bluebell ownership

The Bluebell Railway waits to leave London Bridge with its special train of two inspection saloons, heading for a specially built alighting platform at Hill Place Viaduct on 8 September 1992. MIKE ESAU

Following discussions that had taken place for some time, the handing over of the viaduct to the Bluebell Railway took place with due ceremony on 8 September 1992.

Guests assembled at London Bridge to join a special train formed of the Network SouthEast inspection saloon and the former GWR saloon No 9004, owned by Nick Dodson of Railfilms, hauled by No 73133, the day being orchestrated by Neil Howard of NSE press office. On arrival at a specially constructed platform at the viaduct, John Nelson, managing director NSE explained that with the government white paper on the future of the rail network very much to the fore, the time was right to offer the viaduct and other BR owned structures to the Bluebell Railway. Bernard Holden replied with thanks on behalf of the railway.

A month before Bernard Holden collected his well-deserved MBE, he accepted Hill Place Viaduct on behalf of the railway from John Nelson, managing director of Network South East. MIKE ESAU

Hill Place Viaduct spans the link between town and countryside south of East Grinstead, seen on 23 February 2010. PHILIP LANE PHOTOGRAPHY

The waterproof membrane being installed on the viaduct with ballast being laid on top, autumn 2009. NIGEL LONGDEN

Looking south on the viaduct, with rails being laid on 20 February 2010. JON BOWERS

In BR ownership, Imberhorne Viaduct provided a long siding for the berthing of DEMU stock. A rare passenger train working saw the Branch Line Society's 'Imberhorne Railtour' traverse the viaduct with Hastings Unit No 1031 in the afternoon of 17 September 1983. PHIL BARNES

Landfill Tax Credits

The Bluebell Railway joined the environmental body Entrust and was fortunate enough to receive £100,000 and later £200,000 in the form of Landfill Tax Credits. It was once thought that this stream of funding would finance the removal of waste from Imberhorne Cutting but waste operators were changing the rules and the railway was not at the point where it could guarantee tip clearance by any given date. The funding received was assigned to restoring the viaduct and the feasibility study undertaken for removal of the tip.

'Landfill Tax' was to raise its head again in 2011 regarding the removal of waste from the cutting, when the Landfill Tax Exemption Scheme deadline ended on 1 April 2012 and would have cost the railway much more per ton to move the waste if not met.

Harry Habets, managing director of UK Waste Management Ltd, presents a cheque for £200,000 to Bluebell Railway plc chairman Graham Flight in September 1998. UKWM

Graffiti clearance:
Hill Place Viaduct

by John Sisley

Some of the graffiti on the viaduct's 8ft high parapet walls had been there for decades. This was the view looking north on 22 August 1998. MIKE ESAU

I n December 2005 a copy of *Civic News* – the official newsletter of East Grinstead town council – dropped through my home letter box.

This was given its usual cursory glance; but this time eyes were drawn to an article explaining the merits of a new machine being used by the council which blasted away graffiti without damaging old brickwork.

The removal of graffiti on the internal parapet walls of Hill Place Viaduct was a problem the Bluebell needed to address. In 2005 a group of volunteers from the Northern Extension Team were involved with cleaning out old mortar from the brickwork on the viaduct and then repointing. The graffiti problem was forever staring us in the face. The repointing work was a very long and monotonous process; one which took well over a year to complete. The viaduct is 262 yards long and the parapet walls are 8ft high.

The possible solution to the removal of the graffiti was discussed by the team and it was agreed that we should approach the town council to see if it was prepared to give us a demonstration. Hopefully its new operation would deal with the graffiti on our viaduct brickwork.

On 7 December 2005 a letter was sent to town clerk Chris Rolley to see if the council would be willing to help or advise us. His reply was both swift and encouraging and a demonstration was arranged for 15 December. A particularly bad area was chosen for the experiment and we were

Washing down the chemicals applied to the graffiti.
JOHN SISLEY

BRPS chairman Roy Watts gets 'hands on' on Imberhorne Viaduct on 25 September 2002. MIKE ESAU

Repointing the top of the eastern wall up to capping stone level gives an idea of the extent of the one-time graffiti problem. TONY SULLIVAN

all pleased to see how successful the process proved to be. Some of the graffiti had been on the walls for several years, if not decades.

It would be prudent to explain how the process works. The revolutionary cleaning system was invented in Australia and had already been trialled successfully elsewhere in the UK (mainly by local councils). The area to be cleaned has a non-toxic, chemically-based solution brushed on to it which harmlessly penetrates the brickwork to dissolve paint. After a period of 45 minutes, this is washed away with warm water through a low pressure hose. It is quite harmless and it leaves the surface appearance untouched. Graffiti Removal Ltd (GRL) of Hampshire hold the UK franchise.

A report of the demonstration results was sent to Bluebell infrastructure director Chris White who agreed that we should pursue matters to see how we could best manage to clear the complete viaduct. During his visit to the demonstration, Chris Rolley was taken on his first walk from the viaduct to Hill Place Bridge. He was obviously impressed with all the work the extension team were doing.

We initially thought our team could do all the work but we were immediately advised that a full training programme organised by GRL would be needed, which was expensive. There was also concern, on safety issues, of Bluebell volunteers handling the three chemicals involved.

The council discussed various options with GRL and on 21 December it was confirmed that as Bluebell was a voluntary organisation trying to undertake a difficult and costly task, that GRL would only charge for the chemicals used and send its operatives to East Grinstead. The cost was estimated to be between £1,500 and £2,000. This was recognised by everyone as a very generous offer which Chris White was happy to accept. GRL had been sent some photographs of the state of the walls and it was not expected that the work would be completed in a day.

A meeting was held at the council offices at East Court, East Grinstead, on 5 January between Chris Rolley, Martin Duckworth (EGTC), Ian Aitken (BRPS treasurer) and the writer. The finer points regarding the procedure of payment and covering paperwork was agreed and a date of 18 January for the work to be commenced was fixed. It was agreed that EGTC would liaise with GRL, to confirm the final details. Martin Duckworth was extremely helpful liaising with GRL and ourselves.

GRL was anxious that its offer to assist was given publicity and Barry Coward (Bluebell publicity officer) was contacted and he made the necessary arrangements.

18 January dawned cold but bright and the enthusiasm of their two teams and the town council operatives (Mark, Norman and Steve) was a joy to behold. Nigel Longdon was on site to witness the scene, and later helped to answer the many questions put forward by our visitors. As the morning progressed the press arrived both local (*Courier* and *Observer* – there were two local papers at this time) and the county *Argus* were intrigued to see what was going on. All the consequent newspaper reports (with photographs) were very positive.

Barry Coward was excellent in dealing with numerous questions asked of him.

Chris Rolley, Martin Duckworth, Bernard Gillbard (the town's mayor) and Simon Kerr (East Grinstead tourist officer) were also on site during the day. In the afternoon Matt Starling from West Sussex County Council paid a visit to the site and showed a great deal of interest.

Work continued all day and to everyone's amazement the whole area of the parapet walls was clear of graffiti when the sun finally set. As mentioned above we thought that some walls would be left which EGTC said it would clear at some future date.

So in just over a month from reading *Civic News*, the project was completed very much to the railway's satisfaction.

It must be recorded that the support we had from GRL's personnel, Steve Poole and Quentin Wallace-Jones was very much appreciated. I think that they thoroughly enjoyed themselves and the banter on the day helped to make a long day seem short.

Personally the day will be remembered for the enthusiasm shown by everyone on site, whether a worker or visitor.

Contractors' plant repairing one of the arches on 25 September 2002. MIKE ESAU

Railways to
East Grinstead

A short history
by Graham Poore

It took the Bluebell Railway 43 years to reinstate the line from Horsted Keynes to East Grinstead and, by coincidence, that is the amount of time it took the residents of East Grinstead from lobbying for the town's first railway, to celebrating the opening of the line from the county capital of Lewes into the town – the line that was to become the Bluebell Railway.

In 1839 the railway from London to Croydon opened, and by 1841 trains were running through to Brighton. At this time the population of East Grinstead was only 3586.

With seemingly insignificant places like Haywards Heath and Godstone now having a railway service, it became clear East Grinstead would be left behind. The town's important market was in decline. Although people thought nothing of walking the seven miles to Godstone or Three Bridges it was an altogether tougher problem to get produce, cattle and bulky items over such difficult and hilly ground.

By 1843 farmers and traders could see the business case for a line to Godstone to join the South Eastern Railway's main line from London to Dover, while some of the gentry prefered a line to Three Bridges on the London to Brighton Railway. Both railway companies were lobbied and went to Parliament in 1845 with their rival bills but in 1846 East Grinstead withdrew support for the Godstone option after the South Eastern Railway decided, after an initial survey, that East Grinstead station would be built near Hackenden.

This survey showed the hilly terrain would call for huge expenditure to get the station nearer the town market. A public meeting on 4 March 1846 protested against this alteration but the South Eastern Railway would not give in and local support was withdrawn. A few days later the Brighton Company's bill passed a committee of the House of Commons and the South Eastern Company was rejected. The Brighton Company would build a station at London Road – a very short distance from the important town market and near the centre of what was hoped to become a much larger town.

At this time the railway age was descending into financial meltdown. The London Brighton &

The much-altered and extended first station building at East Grinstead survives and now houses a chiropractic clinic. COLIN TYSON

U1 No 31902 arrives at East Grinstead with a train from Brighton to Victoria in early 1955. MIKE ESAU

C2X No 32440 waiting to leave East Grinstead for Lewes during the 'sulky service' period between the two line closures on 28 December 1955. MIKE ESAU

South Coast Railway (LBSCR) put its resident engineer on unpaid leave and pawned some of its locomotives in an attempt to stay in business and any thought of investing in a railway to East Grinstead was quickly shelved. This seriously upset the plans for the town and the town's relationship with the LBSCR was at rock bottom. A large number of signatures were obtained on a petition requesting the House of Lords not to grant any further approvals for the LBSCR to build any further railways until after it had completed the line to East Grinstead.

Clearly the vested interests in the large railway companies would not be subject to any form of blackmail from East Grinstead residents and at a meeting in 1852 the residents of East Grinstead decided to go it alone and build the line themselves and not rely on another company. They formed a company called The East

Grinstead Railway Co, raised the capital, went to Parliament and got their bill provisionally approved in May 1853, the Act finally passed both Houses in July, tenders were issued and the contract let to George Wythes of Reigate. Wythes was a recognised and successful contractor but it is interesting to read from McDermott's 1886 book about how Wythes tendered in the early days of railway construction; I quote as follows: "If engineers differed so widely it is not surprising that contractors should have gone largely on guess-work, and a story is told of the well-known contractor, the late Mr Wythes, in the early days of railway making, tendering for a contract for an important piece of railway work in this country. He at first thought that about £18,000 would be a remunerative price, and, on consulting, like a prudent man, with his wife, it was agreed to put in a tender for £20,000.

"Thinking it over, however, they agreed that it would not be well to run any risk, and that £40,000 would be a safer figure; and after sleeping over it the wife said: 'I think you had better say £80,000 just to be on the safe side.' This sensible advice was followed, the tender was by far the lowest sent in, and, being accepted, formed the foundation for the vast fortune which Mr Wythes subsequently amassed."

The first excavation took place at a ceremony in East Grinstead in November 1853 and the first locomotive passed into East Grinstead in June 1855. The construction had cost £53,000 to Wythes (it's interesting to speculate how much of this was down to his wife?) and other costs increased the total to £60,000 of which £10,000 was raised by debentures and £50,000 by shares of £25 each. The LBSCR was in favour of the line and agreed to pay £2000 per year rental and

East Grinstead station in 1882, seen from the connecting lines between high level and low level stations, now the site of Sainsbury's store.
EAST GRINSTEAD MUSEUMS

E4 No 32475 at East Grinstead with the 12.28pm football excursion to Lewes on 28 November 1953. COLIN HOGG

would provide the trains on behalf of the company. It also agreed to purchase the line after 10 years following completion and in 1865 paid £53,000. Consequently, the shareholders did not get all their investment back. During the 10 years of ownership the dividends paid to shareholders were very poor – the most ever being paid was about £2 – 90%.

However, the town now had a well-built railway, London was less than 90 minutes away and from Three Bridges it was possible to join fast trains to all parts of the Sussex coast. It is reasonable to assume that at about 1856 some form of commuting from East Grinstead to London commenced and that has now grown to about 1.4 million journeys per year to and from East Grinstead station. The original 1855 station house still survives, although extended, and can be seen from Beeching Way.

On 9 July 1855 public trains commenced running with the first train out of East Grinstead at 12.15pm. Six trains were run and hundreds of people were carried free of charge to celebrate the great occasion. All shops closed at noon, the Brighton Railway band attended, church bells were rung, flags were flown and a great day of festivities took place including a banquet for 200 people held on the lawn of one of the directors.

To work the line a 0-4-2 saddle tank locomotive was built and it was the main power used from 1855 to 1866 when the extension to Tunbridge Wells required a larger engine with more water and coal capacity. The crew were completely exposed to the weather. From Lough's book about the priest extraordinary, the Reverend John Neale, we see in a letter Neale wrote a few days before the line was opened: "I was interrupted by a message that an engine was at the station and I might have a ride to Three Bridges if I liked. I went down, and we ran over in 12 minutes. Just fancy that. Riding on an engine is unspeakably delightful."

So with the start of a daily train service the horse-drawn coach and its five-hour journey to London quickly ceased operation, in under 90 minutes at lower cost the train would win every time. Third class, while cheap, had carriages little better than cattle trucks and it is recorded that every year one would encounter a cheery party of Welsh drovers riding in one of these vehicles on the first stage of their journey home, having walked with their cattle from Wales to East Grinstead for the annual stock fair. So from an isolated small town on the edge of a great forest, East Grinstead suddenly appeared on railway maps and travel of long distances could be done quickly and relatively cheaply.

LINE WEST A SUCCESS

There is no doubt the line was a success, the LBSCR board recorded "the policy pursued by the directors has been attended with beneficial results as regards the East Grinstead line". The working timetables for 1859 show that there were now eight passenger trains per day in each direction and a goods train started running daily. The one intermediate station at Rowfant had been added to by building a station in 1860 in Crawley Down which was called Grange Road.

A railway from Lewes to Uckfield opened for traffic in 1858, the people of Uckfield not wanting to be left behind by East Grinstead and its new railway. Even on the opening day in 1855 the residents of East Grinstead were hoping the line could be extended to Tunbridge Wells and they eventually got the bill through parliament in 1862 for construction of the "East Grinstead, Groombridge & Tunbridge Wells Railway". Meanwhile the line from Uckfield was also to be extended to Tunbridge Wells, before both lines were opened they were taken over by the LBSCR. The Brighton Company was seriously motivated by the fear of the South Eastern Railway encroaching on its territory and building lines to compete for traffic to Brighton, Eastbourne, Newhaven and so on. One can assume that attack being a good form of defence motivated the Brighton Company to seek a share of the traffic from Tunbridge Wells which was then solely South Eastern territory. It provided significant assistance in pushing the bill through parliament.

East Grinstead raised £75,000 and the new company was authorised to borrow up to another £25,000 with Lord West and the Earl de la Warr, both being of the Sackville family, being subscribers. The earl, who had property at Withyham made sure the company built a station and siding for his use at Withyham and this required a signal box to be built, which now resides at Sheffield Park on the Bluebell Railway as part of its museum. The contractor appointed for construction was John Watson & Co of London and work started in July 1863 and no problems were expected, for most of the country through which the line would pass was easy from an engineering point of view – the one exception being the approach from the Medway Valley at Forest Row to the High Weald at East Grinstead.

This required a steep grade and the provision of two short tunnels one of 78 yards under College Lane through sandstone and the other of 48 yards under Lewes Road mainly through clay. One man was killed in a clay land slip and another killed at Withyham after being run over by a wagon. Explosives were used to blast a way through the cutting and the company was fined by East Grinstead Magistrates for storing the explosives too close to the town and just 100 yards from Chequer Mead School. After three years the line was still not completed and according to the *Sussex Express*, "nearly everyone in the town is now looking anxiously for news about our new line, which is to make this town a large city and the centre of attraction to all this side of the Thames".

READY FOR INSPECTION

The LBSCR expected the line to be ready for inspection by the Board of Trade and during the first inspection in July 1866 a list of work still to be done was given and opening refused. A second inspection in August also resulted in failure but eventually the line opened for traffic in October 1866. From my own point of view I have always failed to understand why East Grinstead was so keen on building a line to Tunbridge Wells. During the period that I was familiar with it, from the late 1950s until its closure in 1967 it never seemed to carry any significant numbers of passengers.

Opening of the line in 1866 was ignored by the local press. The line had become a standing joke in Tunbridge Wells and the initial train service was poor. At the LBSCR board meeting in February 1869 it was remarked that 15 years ago the railway was a prosperous concern but thanks to its building useless lines at ruinous cost it no longer was so.

It is interesting to note that in 1966 British Railways released figures showing that ticket sales at East Grinstead the previous year were an average of 300 per day to Three Bridges and 25 per day to Tunbridge Wells. In 1869 the LBSCR produced figures for six months traffic of income of £3033 and operating costs of £3533 thus showing a six month loss of £500. Not a good result for a total capital cost which eventually amounted to an astonishing £174,046.

The area of the original station at East Grinstead was now converted into a useful spacious goods yard and a new through station built across the railway at the London Road Bridge. Similar design to the one seen today at

An engineers' possession on the up line at East Grinstead in the late 1960s. TERRY SHEARING

Eridge. So we now have a new station with trains going west to Three Bridges in one direction and east to Tunbridge Wells in the other. The town started to grow quickly. The rateable value of property in East Grinstead in 1864 was £16,380, in 1874 it grew to £19,932, by 1884 it was £28,741 and 1894 £41,540. This prosperity caused many traders and residents to consider the need for a north and south line to complement their east west line.

Rivalry between the SER and the LBSCR remained intense with both sides desperately trying to defend their territory. In 1864 it was proposed by the Brighton Company to provide financial support to an enterprise called the

Surrey & Sussex Junction Railway and subscribe £500,000 towards the project. This line received its Act in July 1865 and was to run from Croydon via Oxted and Edenbridge to Groombridge and Tunbridge Wells to join with the lines from Uckfield and East Grinstead and traversed South Eastern territory between Croydon and Edenbridge. The South Eastern responded with a proposal for a line from London to Lewes and Brighton and for once joined forces with its Kentish rivals the London Chatham & Dover Railway. This never got through parliament plus the Chatham lost interest.

A contractor called Waring commenced construction and a good deal of heavy

BR No 80145 waiting to leave East Grinstead with a 'sulky service' train to Lewes in 1957. Note the train to Three Bridges waiting in the high level station.
MIKE ESAU

BR No 80152 running round its one LBSCR coach 'sulky service' train at East Grinstead prior to returning to Lewes in 1957. MIKE ESAU

One of the train staff fixing the farewell wreath on to the smokebox of No 80154 prior to it leaving East Grinstead with the last down train to Lewes on 16 March 1958. MIKE ESAU

engineering was done including the 2261 yard long Oxted tunnel. Two shorter tunnels were bored and a substantial four arch brick viaduct at Woldingham was completed. However, construction came to a halt. There were some problems over land deals, labour troubles, a major bank went bankrupt and renewed war between the two main railway companies so the Brighton Company requested it stop construction but was refused with a penalty of £50 per day for failing to complete the line with a limit of £32,250. It was at that time financially in difficulties mainly as a result of expenditure on unprofitable lines and chose to pay the penalty, consequently the Surrey & Sussex Junction Railway effectively ceased to exist. Trees grew and the half finished railway was quietly forgotten and lay hidden in the undergrowth.

Meanwhile, the residents of East Grinstead were happy with the service to Three Bridges and the fast trains from there to London but some years later enthusiasm to have a new line south to Lewes and then on to Brighton coincided with the privately sponsored Lewes and East Grinstead Railway which was launched at a meeting in

Lewes chaired by Lord Sheffield in 1876. Unable to raise all the necessary capital they accepted a takeover by a now more financially stable LBSCR. The highly respected and successful contractor Joseph Firbank was awarded the contract and work was under way in 1878.

It is stated in the Firbank biography that it was an easy line to build with only three notable structures. A brick six arch viaduct south of Horsted Keynes on the short branch to Haywards Heath and a magnificent 10 arch red brick viaduct at Hill Place south of East Grinstead (commonly known today as Imberhorne Viaduct). A tunnel at Sharpthorne of 732 yards was built through treacherous ground and had to be built of extra strength.

When the Board of Trade inspected the line and these structures in particular, the inspector stated that he had: "never seen work better done". Firbank used a Mr T H Myres of Preston as the architect for design of each station who chose soft warm colours and a design in what has become known as the Queen Anne School. Study of the stations on the Bluebell Railway show what a fine design was chosen.

When Firbank started construction there remained questions about whether or not a line from the north would ever arrive at East Grinstead. He made sure the line from the south came off Hill Place viaduct pointing in the London direction but was forced to order design and materials for a three track bridge over Glen View Road (later renamed Railway Approach) to allow for the trains from Lewes to enter the second East Grinstead station at London Road. Very soon after this, an Act was passed for the Croydon, Oxted & East Grinstead Railway. Half a railway already existed between Croydon and Oxted and the Brighton and South Eastern agreed to a friendly relationship and to share the line from Croydon to Crowhurst.

The SER would have a connection with its old mainline which ran from Redhill to Tonbridge and Dover. South of Crowhurst the line to East Grinstead would be exclusively the Brighton and would make an end on connection with the line coming up from Lewes. Firbank was awarded this contract as well. In 1866 when the major bank of Overend, Gurney & Co went bankrupt with liabilities of £10 million, the Brighton like many other companies was seriously affected by panic and the directors had to ask Firbank to forgo many of his claims for payment. He agreed to take part payment in shares at par which fell within a few months to 38%. However, he refused to sell having full confidence in the Brighton Company and was rewarded by a substantial premium some years later. One can speculate that his cooperation with the Brighton when it was in difficulty played an important part in his winning many substantial contracts including the Lewes to East Grinstead line.

Samuel Laing, chairman of the LBSCR at a meeting in 1886 referring to Firbank's death in June that year said: " I believe he never skimped a bit of work in his life, but in all contracts he has had with us we have had good honest work for our money. I only say these few words as a tribute to his memory and to express regret that we and a great many of us feel that he is not here, as he has been accustomed to be, today."

With Firbank now nearing completion of the line from Lewes to East Grinstead and being awarded the contract from Croydon to East Grinstead, he had the engineers design what would be the third station at East Grinstead.

It was important that the east west line and north south line shared the same station for convenient interchanges but they would be at

View to the low level station from the high level. TERRY SHEARING

The steps from high level to low level. TERRY SHEARING

different levels and at nearly 90º to each other so a two level station was designed.

The Brighton Company was very aware that the line from Lewes passed through very isolated country and while goods traffic was expected to be good, passenger traffic was likely to be light. As a consequence, it wanted the option for trains from London to either head south to Lewes or alternatively make their way to the high level platform to proceed to Tunbridge Wells. So a line was built from the high level station to a location a mile north of East Grinstead at Hackenden, named St Margaret's Junction after a nearby convent, this joined with the low level line on its way to Oxted and London. The St Margaret's line was on such a tight curve it was later to severely restrict the size of locomotive that could use it.

While excited by the pending arrival of the north south lines, the residents were unhappy that the station was being moved from London Road a fairly significant distance to the east. The parish magazine said: "The distance of the new station from the town is much felt and it is to be hoped that the roads and approaches will be speedily improved." The town council is still saying it would like the road from the station to the town centre improved 130 years later. In a 1885 book about East Grinstead W Pepper comments: "The station which was recently built is a very commodious and convenient structure with handsome and spacious buildings for the accommodation of both passengers and officials. There are embankments on the outside planted with shrubs and flowers which, when in full foliage and blossom, present a very showy appearance. The drive up to the entrance is well arranged, a centre clump of plants with lamp, forming a useful and at the same time, pleasing object."

The old order changeth: In this undated view of circa 1972 the Myres designed station house has been swept away and its replacement 'CLASP' structure is well advanced in its construction, as is the new concrete footbridge. At the same time, gas lighting has given way to modern electric lamp standards and the days of the up side canopy and retaining wall are numbered. COLIN TYSON COLLECTION

By August 1882 the line from Lewes to East Grinstead (London Road) had apart from some goods handling facilities, been completed and trains started to run between East Grinstead and Brighton. Construction of the high level platforms involved the realignment of the line from Three Bridges. This arrived in nearly a straight line into the London Road station and it was necessary to change the course of the line a quarter of a mile before the high level platforms so that it arrived in the right place. The service from Three Bridges was not affected during construction.

The high level had two island platforms. These were not as splendid as the main station building on the lower level but both had refreshment rooms. Strangely, no water facilities for the locomotives were provided at either level despite the fact that a water supply had been provided at the London Road station. This stopped being used after the double-deck station opened and it was some 40 years before a water tower from

A busy scene at East Grinstead High Level on 1 January 1967, the last day of service from Three Bridges to Tunbridge Wells. The first train of the day (9.08am) arrives from Three Bridges and its signalling token collected, thus allowing the 8.55am from Tunbridge Wells (in the station) to continue to Grange Road and Three Bridges. JOHN VAUGHAN

The same view upon closure. TERRY SHEARING

The last surviving signal box at East Grinstead was 'C' box, often worked by Bluebell member Clive Emsley in its latter years, who switched the box out for the last time. It was demolished upon electrification of the line, the 'branch' now being worked completely from Oxted panel. MIKE ESAU

Streatham was moved to East Grinstead and erected at the London end of Platform five. Only trains from Tunbridge Wells to London could take water at East Grinstead. Passenger access from one low level platform to the other was by a covered footbridge. Access to the four high level platforms was by stairways from either low level platform. With completion of the line to Oxted, trains commenced running in 1884 and a service of four trains a day was provided between London and Brighton. The St Margaret's loop was not used until late 1885.

Firbank is reported as implying that the original work done by Warings for the Surrey & Sussex Junction Railway was probably more of a hindrance to him than building the line from scratch. Of particular interest to me was Firbank's decision to go for wrought-iron lattice girder structures on brick piers for the three large viaducts on the line from Croydon to East Grinstead, the finest of these is a mile or two north of East Grinstead across a small lake known as Cook's Pond. It has five spans each 125ft wide with a brick arch of 12ft at each abutment and an extra elliptical arch of 30ft span at the southern end. The height from the lake to the rails is about 65ft. A footpath exists near this viaduct and a fine view is possible of this magnificent structure.

With north south and east west trains now running, work was completed on goods facilities. A substantial goods yard south and east of the low level platforms was completed with much siding and ground storage space. The high level yard was altered slightly and the three tracks of the spur up from Hill Place Viaduct were no longer used for passenger trains with one becoming the link from low to high level the others becoming useful extra siding space, although their use was later limited due to the steep gradient and fear of trucks without brakes running away to the south. In 1884 a private siding was built a mile or so west of East Grinstead on the line to Three Bridges to serve a significant house and farm on the Imberhorne Estate at Gulledge. When Major General Hutchinson carried out the Board of Trade inspection he raised concerns that a truck could run away on the 1-in-94 falling grade towards Grange Road and decided to try an

A Class 377 EMU arrives at East Grinstead from London Victoria.
COLIN TYSON

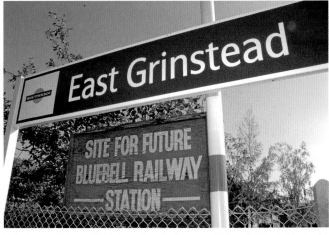

This sign proclaiming Bluebell's extremely 'long-term' interest at East Grinstead stood for nearly three decades by the down platform fence. COLIN TYSON

experiment. They released a truck and found it stopped considerably short of Grange Road. William Stenning who owned a significant timber business in Sussex and was a director of the original 1853 company, had a siding built from the high level into his extensive timber yard and he also had a narrow gauge railway for moving large tree trunks.

With steep climbs of up to 1-in-70 the line from Croydon to East Grinstead would be slow. It is interesting that despite the direct line from London to East Grinstead via Oxted being opened in 1884 many still preferred to travel on the local to Three Bridges and change to the fast trains from there to London. A slip coach service operated from 1888 until 1932 whereby an express from London slipped a coach at Horley or Three Bridges which the onboard guard stopped at the station and a loco then hauled it to East Grinstead. But it can be seen that the railways at East Grinstead showed little change for the first 20 years. Trains ran from Three Bridges to Tunbridge Wells and from Brighton to London and as a general rule were designed to be in East Grinstead at the same time to allow interchange.

By 1905 some quite reliable double deck motor buses began to operate and while the LBSCR had nothing to fear from this new competition initially, as concerned East Grinstead, it was mindful in other areas of the need to provide frequent services at a lower operating cost. A small loco and one coach was tried with some success and a small halt (station) was built at Hurst Green between Lingfield and Oxted. As the years passed by and traffic on the line to the south became even less, more trains from London made use of the St Margaret's spur and continued on to Tunbridge Wells instead of Lewes and Brighton. Also, trains arriving from London could use the goods spur to the high level and be facing the right way to return to London.

In 1921 the South Eastern & Chatham Railway proposed to electrify many lines and this would include the line from London Bridge to Oxted and Crowhurst Junction near Lingfield and promised a 40% increase in train speeds, however, the financial state of the various railway companies after the war was such that the government decided the numerous small railway companies should be amalgamated into various large groups. The resulting Southern Railway would include the LBSCR and SECR plus the LSWR which ran as far west as Cornwall. Many of today's commuters do not realise that back in 1920 as their train from East Grinstead joined the mainline at South Croydon the whole railway was covered in overhead electric cables and masts all the way to London Bridge.

The Southern Railway extended third rail electrification from the suburban lines around London to Lewes, Brighton, Eastbourne, Worthing and Hastings in the 1930s and it planned a local service from Seaford to Horsted Keynes. Horsted Keynes was chosen for terminating the electric Seaford trains rather than occupy platform space at the extremely busy Haywards Heath. It is recorded that the Southern planned to extend electrification from Horsted Keynes through East Grinstead and up to Croydon but the war put an end to this idea.

In September 1939 five days after war was declared, bureaucracy swung into action, timetables changed, blackouts, blast protection, carriage windows covered in a type of plastic

The steel and concrete 'CLASP' (Consortium of Local Authorities Special Programme) building in Southern livery October 2005. COLIN TYSON

Looking north at East Grinstead in 2010, prior to the platforms being extended northwards to accommodate longer trains. PHIL BARNES

Making the interchange obvious to passengers. COLIN TYSON

The era between steam and electric at East Grinstead was largely worked by DEMU. Unit No 205015 waits to leave for London on February 1, 1987, the year of electrification. **MIKE ESAU**

material with a diamond shaped hole so that passengers could peer out to see where they were, but soon after this, station names were taken down to prevent invaders or low flying aircraft knowing where they were. White lines were painted on platform edges and stripes on vertical columns in the hope people would see them in the enforced darkness. Within a few months things returned to normal and the railways in East Grinstead passed a fairly uneventful war.

The same cannot be said of the town. Forest Row station had been slightly damaged by a German bomb but on 9 July 1943 a German bomber strafed Dormans station and a train there, then dropped two 500kg and eight 50kg high explosive bombs across East Grinstead killing 108 people and injuring 235 – one third were children in the Whitehall cinema.

Official peace celebrations took place in the summer of 1946 but the war had taken its toll on the railways. Upon nationalisation in 1948 the Southern Railway became the Southern Region of British Railways and East Grinstead was part of the central section which approximately equated to the old LBSCR.

In 1955 the line south to Lewes was closed, it was claimed to be unprofitable. The train timetable for East Grinstead was recast to provide a regular interval service. By this means one knew trains left Victoria during the day at eight minutes past every hour. A train to London and a train to Tunbridge Wells plus one to Three Bridges were all timed to be at the high level station at the same time every hour. Apart from a few evening rush hour arrivals which used the low level platform so as to turn for departure back to

London, the low level fell into disuse. Closure of the line from East Grinstead to Lewes caused an outcry and it was discovered by local resident Miss Madge Bessemer that British Railways would need an Act of Parliament to close the line and was forced to reopen it.

It ran the minimum number that was required

16,000 people travelled on East Grinsteads Electrification Gala Weekends held on 26-27 September 1987.

by the original Act of four trains each way per day. One coach was sufficient and few people used the so-called 'sulky service', which didn't call at Kingscote or Barcombe as they had not been mentioned in the original Act. The line finally closed in 1958 but remained operational for special traffic until 1960. It was now clear that substantial amounts of tax payers' money was being lost on the railway and something needed to be done.

Dr Richard Beeching was born in Maidstone, Kent, in 1913, attended a local grammar school and obtained a first class honours degree in physics followed by a research PhD. It was clear he had an outstanding ability for research; he had a good sense of humour and was generally well liked. In 1948 he joined ICI and in 1960 joined a committee who was charged with the task of looking at the terrific losses being incurred by the British Transport Commission who had control of the railways. In 1961 he was appointed chairman of British Railways. He lived in East Grinstead, his house was on Lewes Road, and commuted to work in London each day by train. He caught the 8.35am which arrived at Victoria at 9.38am and every effort was made to ensure the train arrived on time.

Two Standard Class 4 4-6-0 locos were allocated to Three Bridges shed, Nos 75075 and 75070, these being the largest available that could use the sharp curve of St Margaret's loop. He always sat in the same first class compartment with a group of other senior business people. I was told by one loco driver that he always acknowledged the crew at Victoria. The task of getting the chairman to work on time fell to the top link drivers at Three Bridges shed; it

Excavation in progress on 28 February 2012 to lay the foundations for the town's fifth station, during which contractors unearthed the red brick layout of the third station! TIM BAKER

A warmer, brighter and more inviting station building greeted the prospective traveller by December 2012. The old station building behind is fenced off and was awaiting demolition after removal of asbestos. COLIN TYSON

was hard work getting the heavy train to Victoria in one hour three minutes while stopping at nearly all stations. Staff at each station were briefed on the importance of this particular train and it is said the platform staff were blowing their whistles for the trains' departure even before it had stopped.

By early 1963 Beeching produced a substantial report entitled Reshaping of British Railways. Following two years of research and analysis the report proposed the closure of one third of the country's 7000 stations, the withdrawal of passenger services from 5000 route miles and the loss of 70,000 jobs over three years. It became clear that the line to the south to Lewes would never reopen and tenders for demolition were prepared. The line from Three Bridges through East Grinstead to Tunbridge Wells would also be closed.

My teacher at Imberhorne School, aware of my enthusiasm for trains urged me to write a booklet with some of my friends about the history of the railways in East Grinstead and we sent a copy to Dr Beeching pleading with him not to close the line to Three Bridges. This was a well used and an important line for young people to get to technical college in Crawley and for work people to get to Crawley and the rapidly growing airport at Gatwick.

With closure of the line to Lewes and Brighton, the line to Three Bridges was the only way to travel to the south. BR published figures showing the daily number of passengers from East Grinstead to London was 950, to Three Bridges 300 and to Tunbridge Wells 25. What really annoyed was that BR wanted to look at the line

from Three Bridges to Tunbridge Wells as one line, whereas we argued that the line to Three Bridges should be looked at on its own after all it had been built separately in the first place.

We made one last attempt to prevent closure by contacting the Labour Minister Barbara Castle, but she refused point blank to even discuss the matter.

THE DIESEL ERA

Steam traction at East Grinstead slowly started to give way to diesel electric trains from 1962. An order had been placed for 19 three-car units to be built for the Oxted lines but commuters soon realised they were uncomfortable, the motor coach vibrated (which was not surprising as you could be sitting a few feet away from a 600hp four-cylinder diesel engine) and was noisy and draughts made winter travel a nightmare. They initially proved unreliable although to the great credit of the maintenance teams they soon got to grips with the new trains and reliability improved. At one time reliability was so poor that a spare locomotive was at Oxted waiting to head off to rescue any broken down train. During a spell of daily commuting to London I recall on the high speed run between Oxted and Lingfield, everyone would be forced to stop reading the newspaper as the bouncing up and down and sideways was so violent as to render reading impossible.

Steam traction continued into 1963 and sometimes appeared to cover for a failed diesel train. The two coach service to Three Bridges remained steam hauled for a while after diesel worked the London trains. The last steam train on

the line from Three Bridges to Tunbridge Wells was in June 1965 and the last steam on the line from London via the St Margaret's loop was on 12 December 1966. This reversed at East Grinstead and went to Three Bridges. Ironically, this last BR steam hauled train in East Grinstead was hauled by No 75075 the very engine that took Dr Beeching to work each day.

Insufficient diesel unit trains were built so three rush hour trains were to be hauled by a class three diesel electric locomotive hauling eight Mk.1 corridor coaches. If possible East Grinstead commuters tried to use these trains as they were very comfortable, soft riding and well heated. The coaches were kept overnight in sidings at East Grinstead, one set sat on Hill Place viaduct. Locos came down very early each morning and with engines running they electrically heated the coaches much to the annoyance of Garden Wood residents who were woken up early by all the noise and activity.

As early as 1952 a diesel loco had been tried at East Grinstead but proved to be underpowered for the steep inclines and very unreliable. The Southern Region did not have any electrically heated coaches initially so some were borrowed or acquired from the Western Region. Some of the steam heated coaching stock was hauled by diesel locos but unheated of course. This resulted in near riots at East Grinstead. Some goods type vans with a small oil fired boiler were tagged on to the back of the trains but did not heat the trains sufficiently.

After 25 years' service the diesel units were beginning to be worn out and engineers reported in 1980 that if the units were not replaced by

The official opening of Network Rail's new East Grinstead station building on Friday 8 March 2013 whereby Chris White, Tim Baker, Caroline Collins and Lesley-Anne Liddell represented Bluebell. Seen cutting the ribbon is Mid Sussex MP Nicholas Soames in the company of Cllr Liz Bennett mayor of East Grinstead, Southern Railway MD Chris Burchell and Mark Ruddy Network Rail's Sussex route manager. TIM BAKER

1987 the line from East Grinstead to London would have to close as the trains would be unsafe to operate. In 1983 BR announced that electrification would take place to East Grinstead at a cost of £7 million. By July 1987 the first electric train arrived in East Grinstead. Work had mainly been done on Sundays when the line was closed.

Rather like the celebrations in 1855 when the first train arrived in East Grinstead, 26-27 September 1987 saw celebrations at most stations along the East Grinstead line. The Bluebell Railway sent one of its locos by road to display at East Grinstead, three locos were displayed at Oxted and the disused signal box at Lingfield was opened to the public. The old diesel units were still to run back and forth from Uckfield to Oxted until new diesel trains were available as money for electrification from Oxted to Uckfield could not be found. The celebrations were a big success with 16,000 people travelling on a £1 ticket for freedom of the whole line, including to Uckfield.

The last passenger train on the high level station was in January 1967 and even before track lifting started, the county council was advising that an inner relief road would be built to reduce traffic jams in the town centre. It always struck me as suspicious that the line from East Grinstead to Three Bridges which could easily have been made to pay its way, was sacrificed for the council's road scheme.

When this inner relief road was eventually built and opened in 1978 a suggested name in view of the deep cutting the road was built in, was Beeching Cut, but this was rejected one presumes on political grounds and it was named Beeching Way.

The high level station was demolished and a large car park built and in 1971 the LBSCR station building was demolished with many of the cast iron fittings and nameboards going to America for use in the Victoria Station themed steakhouse restaurants.

The replacement station (station number four) of a small prefabricated 'CLASP' type structure with very limited facilities was built and later a Sainsbury's supermarket built on the low level goods yard. This station building was in turn demolished in 2012 and an improved station building erected and officially opened on 8 March 2013 (station number five). With the withdrawal of all slam door carriage stock a few years ago, East Grinstead now enjoys the service of Class 377 Electrostar trains and the recent lengthening of the platforms (under the long-running Thameslink programme) to allow longer trains should help reduce overcrowding in the rush hour as well as recent improvements to the station car park occupying the old line to Three Bridges being extended upwards by one storey.

Mileposts at East Grinstead: an anomaly explained

Readers might be interested to know that the distance between the Bluebell Railway's platform and the Network Rail platforms at East Grinstead is… 13 miles!

When Network Rail gangs cleared the undergrowth adjacent to the siding/rail connection behind Bluebell's platform on 1 September 2010, they exposed the 17-mile milepost, situated opposite the northern end of our platform. For reference, the 15-mile milepost is at the north end of Kingscote station and is situated on the Up side.

At the northern end of the Southern station's platform two is the 30-mile milepost… but why are they 13 miles apart!

The reason for this anomaly is that mileposts on the Bluebell Line are referenced from the south – Culver Junction – (and are located on the Up side), while mileposts north of East Grinstead are referenced from London Bridge (and are on the Down side).

STEPHEN FAIRWEATHER

Above: The 30-mile milepost at the north of Platform two at East Grinstead.
STEPHEN FAIRWEATHER

Below: The 17-mile milepost opposite the north end of our new platform at East Grinstead.

Network connected!

PROPOSED STATION BUILDING FOR EAST GRINSTEAD *M Thompson 2/93.*

The station that Bluebell didn't have: member Mark Thompson produced this rather fanciful 'art deco' version of how the Bluebell's station at East Grinstead could look. In the end there was neither the space available, or the funding available, although something more substantial facility-wise is still planned for the future.

Looking north and the remnants of the old double track formation south of East Grinstead station to the viaduct are visible in this 1993 scene. MIKE ESAU

The Bluebell P. Way gang tracklaying in January 2009 at East Grinstead to enable the Network Rail physical connection. JON BOWERS

BRPS Chairman Roy Watts, Mac Macintosh, Gordon Pettitt, East Grinstead Mayor Ginnie Waddingham and Bluebell plc chairman Graham Flight at the 4-Vep handover ceremony. JON BOWERS

Ex-BR Southern Region General manager Gordon Pettitt with his namesake unit. JON BOWERS

During 2009 and early 2010 much work was done to enable waste extraction from the tip by rail, which thanks to industry-wide co-operation, became an affordable option.

The track layout planned for the Bluebell platform at East Grinstead was required to accommodate the waste trains (half of the spoil wagons staying in the platform while the locomotive propels the other half of the wagons south to the tip face) and before laying track into the station area, there was the need to build the platform, since that would be almost impossible after tracks were laid. With the completion of the Bluebell platform it was possible to run events and fundraising open days at the station.

One of the major reasons for extending to East Grinstead was to physically join up with the national rail network, thereby facilitating the movement of locomotives and rolling stock and incoming charter trains etc.

To this end the railway was helped enormously by its 'friends in high places' and Network Rail connected Bluebell rails to the main line at East Grinstead on 14 January 2009.

This photo shows clearly the Network Rail connection to Bluebell rails, via a locked gate and is visible on the track circuits with Oxted panel. Note the points levers worked by the ground frame. ANDREW STRONGITHARM

NETWORK CONNECTED!

The visiting tamper is 'parked' on the short siding at East Grinstead on 12 June 2010, just short of the viaduct. STEPHEN FAIRWEATHER

The first open day

Despite the Bluebell's station area at East Grinstead being a construction site, a hugely successful first Open Day was held by the railway on Saturday 17 January 2009 to mark the connection of its line to the national network and to receive celebrity 4-Vep unit No 3417 *Gordon Pettitt* to Bluebell stock.

For its journey from Wimbledon Park depot to East Grinstead, No 3417 was accompanied by Electro-Diesel No 73109 *Battle of Britain* –

50th Anniversary, both being immaculately turned out by South West Trains staff. Bluebell dignitaries joined the train at Clapham Junction.

Propelled by No 73109 on its rear from East Grinstead NR station, No 3417 crossed on to the Bluebell's track – the first train to do so in 45 years.

The unit was then formally presented to Bluebell by South West Trains for a nominal £1.

A total of 730 visitors came to the site to witness the event and with temporary shop and catering sales, a total of just over £4,000 was raised "proving the sort of interest that our arrival from the south will generate" said commercial manager Tim Baker.

The unit remained in Bluebell ownership and returned for further open days whereby passengers could appreciate the novelty of travelling over the viaduct to the buffer stops just north of the tip.

East Grinstead welcomes our 'first train'. The unit was propelled almost to the viaduct gates. MIKE ESAU

4-Vep No 3417 arrives at East Grinstead on 17 January 2009 to an admiring audience. JON BOWERS

EAST GRINSTEAD

Creating the period ambience

by Graham Poore

Initially, consideration was given to an Art Deco station at East Grinstead (page 114), a style popular with the Southern Railway in the 1930s but this plan was frustrated by Network Rail requiring engineering access on land formerly earmarked for the Bluebell station. There was concern among some Bluebell volunteers that another line of thought might be a budget platform with modern street lighting, creosoted fences and a minimal maintenance approach.

Friends of Kingscote (FOK), a long standing group of volunteers, felt that despite the restricted options available at East Grinstead, the platform ought to have a Southern Railway 'flavour' with some reference to the original station. Hence they proposed the manufacture of replicated LBSCR cast iron lamp posts, timber platform fencing, wooden benches and original style Southern enamel signs, all in the 1950s – 1960s Southern Region colour scheme. This would present an appearance similar to how East Grinstead station looked in the early 1960s prior to demolition.

Clearly there would be cost implications and between 1000 and 2000 hours of volunteer labour would be required. Les Haines took on the sourcing of reproduction lamp posts. Desmond O'Neil, a former FOK volunteer, had left over £100,000 in his will specifically towards an 'East Grinstead station', this money being 'ring-fenced' under the control of the Bluebell Railway Trust and it was agreed that the trust would fund the reproduction lamp posts. Two quotations were received and the contract awarded to Hargreaves Foundry of Halifax. A spare original LBSCR lamp post was stripped of paint by Les using much paint stripper and scraping and sent to Hargreaves for mould making.

Old rail uprights and Arris rails in position as the FOK team add the palings to the fence at East Grinstead, with leader of the fixing group, Keith Marriott, centre. ANDREW STRONGITHARM

NETWORK CONNECTED!

Progress

Due to heavy snow over the winter of 2009, withdrawal from working on the northern extension resulted in a five-week setback in the programme, which is unfortunate but unavoidable – we are lucky it was no longer. Good progress is now being made again at East Grinstead with the platform front wall nearing completion, the S&T equipment room in place and track going back on the viaduct. Once the tunnel relaying work is completed, focus will return to tracklaying at East Grinstead station site and southwards to the north end of the cutting. Lots of other essential tasks have been completed as well, including planting to screen the railway from nearby houses, P. Way work, preparation of the ground frames to control the S&C, installation of gates and yet more service ducts put in place.

Chris White, Spring 2010.

Above: The start of platform construction at East Grinstead on 20 February 2010. JON BOWERS

Left: The platform retaining wall to the Network Rail boundary shows the proximity of the platform to the headshunt used by Southern for stock storage. ANDREW STRONGITHARM

Right above: The temporary ticket office at East Grinstead, utilised for the platform opening weekend on 4-5 September. PHIL BARNES

Right below: At the open weekend held at East Grinstead on 4-5 September 2010, 1,488 tickets were sold for a ride on the 4-Vep No 3417 hauled by GBRf Class 73 ED No 73208 *Kirsten*. Trains departed hourly from 10am to 5.10pm.

Replicated LBSCR lamp posts, of the pattern still being used at East Grinstead (when gas lit) until modernisation in the late 1960s. Target signs were manufactured from copying an original and fire buckets add to a period but workable charm. PHIL BARNES

Nine lamps would be required for East Grinstead with two extra for the likely extension of the Sheffield Park platforms. It cost £2500 for the mould and £790 per column plus delivery.

Keith Marriott took on the task of producing the swan necks and electric fittings, together with refurbishment of a set of Southern Region white hexagonal lamp shades, rescued by the late Alan Closs from Burgess Hill station.

A large storage shed at Kingscote, which previously housed the railway's JCB and nicknamed the 'Giraffe House' due to its height, was used to both store the lamp posts and manufacture the platform paling fence.

Covers of Cooksbridge quoted for 1500 palings and an order was duly placed and the palings delivered and stored in the Giraffe House. In addition more than 60 wooden Arris rails were needed for fixing between the vertical fence posts which, in time honoured Southern Railway tradition, are made of recycled bullhead rail secured in a concrete up stand beam. This beam exists mainly to guide rain water into the drainage channel which then goes to a sump, along with water off

the viaduct. This will be pumped into the water storage tank for use by the locos.

A framework of timber was made as a jig for painting and storing the palings and two adjacent containers used for paint drying, the Weathershield flexible paint needing 10 days to fully harden. Requests were put out for help and the FOK team was assisted by volunteers from Infrastructure, Carriage & Wagon, and many more groups and departments. Mindful of the need to reduce future maintenance and consequent costs a high quality job was planned. Each paling would have the edges chamfered as it is impossible to get proper paint coverage on a sharp 90° corner.

Each paling would have knotting compound applied, then a coat of Dulux Aquatech (a combined timber preservative and base coat) two coats of undercoat and one gloss top coat of the correct 'Bamboo' colour, mixed for us by Brewers – the local Dulux distributor.

John Sisley at Kingscote took on the task of coordinating production, finding volunteers and managing delivery of finished components to East Grinstead at the time they were required. Keith Marriott led the fixing

A huge amount of progress has been made at the East Grinstead site over the past few weeks. This has been possible by the combined efforts of the infrastructure teams and contractors involved.

Track installed, complete with switches and crossings, from the north end of the site to about 300 metres north of the infilled cutting face. This includes tamping and alignment by a machine brought in by road late one Sunday evening when Sainsbury's was closed as the road had to be blocked for the movement.

Installation of the two ground frames being provided for local control of the Network Rail connection and engine run-round facilities in an advanced stage of delivery.

Construction of the platform is also at an advanced stage. Delays with delivery of the concrete edging slabs from the supplier has impacted on the programme which is a nuisance but will be recovered.

Fencing, walkways, lamp posts, signs, electrical supply cables and the mobile ticket office are all in the process of being installed with a final inspection of the site by Her Majesty's Railway Inspector scheduled for the end of July.

Chris White, Summer 2010.

group. Traditional oval nails would be used for fixing the paling to the Arris rail. Back at Kingscote, the gloss top coat would be applied to each paling on one face and both edges and after the gloss face was nailed to the Arris rail, the nail was sunk by a punch below the timber surface – the resulting hole filled and then touched up with undercoat. The final topcoat could then be applied to the paling face in situ. This means you cannot see the fixing, which prevents water penetration and prolongs the life of the paling.

The next part of the project was the station nameplates. East Grinstead (Low Level) had retained its Southern Railway 'target' signs until demolition and a tracing of an original surviving example was given to Les Haines by Colin Tyson. Quotations were sought and Stock Signs of Redhill (who supply train operators Southern) were awarded the contract to reproduce the top quality set of vitreous enamel target signs that now adorn East Grinstead's lamp posts.

An original East Grinstead running-in board of SR vintage had already been loaned by the Museum Department and Friends of Kingscote members fabricated its new surround.

Add some flower tubs, fire buckets hanging on their brackets and some poster boards and a suitable railway style ambience has been created from nothing. In 2012 Network Rail offered Bluebell the 1876 Grade II listed signal box at Billingshurst free of charge upon its redundancy under a signalling renewal scheme. The plan is to locate the structure at East Grinstead to further boost the railway atmosphere but not be operational, with all extension signalling ultimately being controlled from Kingscote North.

Hopefully when funds allow, a station canopy will be erected, for which foundation pads have been cast into the platform, and a small building to house a ticket office and toilets.

Original rails and LBSCR brackets make up the 'new' running-in board, complete with an original Southern Railway two-piece enamel sign.
PHIL BARNES

First 'through train' Blue Belle special since 1963

History was made on 6 November 2010 when the Bluebell Railway ran its first direct through 'Blue Belle' charter on to its own metals for the first time since the line was severed from the main network with the closure of the Ardingly branch in 1963.

The railway chartered Hastings Diesels Ltd's preserved DEMU No 1001, running from its Hastings base through to East Grinstead and southwards to the 'tip face' at 'Imberhorne North', via London Bridge and return.

The fundraising trip stopped just briefly at the Network Rail/Bluebell boundary to pick up Bluebell pilotman, Ted Oades, and ran straight to Imberhorne via the restored viaduct.

The train then returned to Bluebell's new platform at East Grinstead, whereby day visitors could continue to use shuttle services provided by No 1001 over the viaduct for the rest of the day before the charter returned to Hastings at 4.30pm.

As part of an open weekend at East Grinstead, the following day saw viaduct shuttles in the hands of visiting GBRf Class 73 No 73141 *Charlotte* – hauling the railway's 4-Vep unit No 3417 *Gordon Pettitt*.

The Hastings Blue Belle
3rd **Special Excursion** 3rd
to Imberhorne North
(East Grinstead)
Via **Hillplace Viaduct**
(subject to Company Bye Laws)
6/11/10
1000

Crossing the viaduct, heading south with the 1.40pm shuttle train.
PHIL BARNES

Arrival at East Grinstead on 6 November 2010, where *Charlotte* and the 4-Vep occupied the adjacent line. Headcode 77 was the London Bridge to East Grinstead code. COLIN TYSON

No 1001 at the north end of the viaduct, with the return of the 10.40am shuttle. PHIL BARNES

'Blue Belle' at the buffers at London Bridge. COLIN TYSON

The road is set for Bluebell at East Grinstead.

Test and training runs

In the short timescale available between the north and south sections of Bluebell Railway being physically connected at Imberhorne Lane Bridge on 8 March 2013 and the opening of public services to East Grinstead on 23 March, training test trains for loco crews, guards and signalmen were run over the new section northwards from Kingscote.

Right: The first 'Bluebell train to East Grinstead' therefore was hauled by BR 9F No 92212 – heading three test/training runs to East Grinstead on Saturday 16 March. This is the first of those trains entering East Grinstead, which, for the record, left Kingscote at 2.20pm and arrived at East Grinstead at 2.30pm. The access from Bluebell to the national network is seen, left, and a Southern train at East Grinstead station.
STEPHEN FAIRWEATHER

Below: The test/training run arrives at East Grinstead on 16 March amid much interest from working members and Northern Extension Project volunteers.
ANDREW STRONGITHARM

Come thou glorious day of promise...

by Colin Tyson
Bluebell News Spring 2013

23 March 2013.

We bought a station site to stop houses being built on it and blocking the route north forever. We applied for planning permission to rebuild our railway another six miles to East Grinstead (the trackbed being split into 31 plots) but planning permission was refused by one vote against. We forced a Public Inquiry and bought a further station. We took on the longest tunnel in preservation and a Grade II listed 10 arch viaduct. We did sponsored walks in the 1980s and another one just last month. We made and sold jam and we sold second-hand railway books. We bought shares in three share issues and we gradually relaid the line – inch by inch. We moved 70,000 tons of domestic waste by road and by rail out of a deep cutting through some dreadful weather – and hit our own deadline to do it to ensure that it didn't cost us more. We forced a promise made to us to safeguard our strip of land at East Grinstead against outside commercial interests, joined up with Network Rail and built a new station at East Grinstead.

When you say it all quickly that was 43 years' worth. And on 23 March passenger trains ran over those triumphant arches into East Grinstead once again.

That is what we did. Every one of our members, volunteers, staff, supporters and shareholders helped to do it.

What we didn't do is borrow money from the bank to complete our Northern Extension, neither did we receive any large grants.

Attitudes change of course over 40 years. Who would have guessed that the very council that refused us planning so long ago, would end up giving us £50,000 towards tip clearance, £25,000 towards the viaduct and £25,000 towards the new water tower?

We can think of even slower projects than this one; our water-loving Surrey and Sussex neighbours of the Wey & Arun Canal Trust still have a long way

Left above: The first passenger timetabled service, the 9.45am 'The Pioneer' train for Sheffield Park, leaves East Grinstead on northern extension opening day, 23 March 2013. DUDLEY HUBBARD

Left: The first ECS train arrives at East Grinstead in a blizzard on 23 March to form 'The Pioneer' 9.45am departure, using three classic Bluebell locomotives of Nos 55 Stepney, 323 Bluebell and B473. ANDREW STRONGITHARM

The historic first passsenger train 'south' waits to depart from East Grinstead on 23 March. STEPHEN FAIRWEATHER

Nos 323 and B473 head the 10.30am 'Grinsteade Pullman' train from East Grinstead past Hill Place Farm Bridge on 24 March. PHIL BARNES

to go to realise their dream and many plots of land still to purchase. There may have been more dramatic and scenic railway projects completed in the meantime; the Welsh Highland Railway rebuilt across Snowdonia springs to mind, but hey, and sorry guys, this is narrow gauge and you did have Millennium Commission funding to kick start your project. To do what we have done in the busy and crowded south east where land is at such a premium, we can hold our heads very high and say…Mission accomplished!

OPENING FESTIVAL

From Saturday 23 March to 7 April 2013 the Bluebell put on another of its grand shows, not seen since the 50th anniversary gala in 2010. We were billed to have BR Standard Class 7 No 70000 *Britannia* but the North Norfolk Railway kindly broke it and so it could not attend. Nevertheless a four-train intensive service supplemented by Pullman trains took the reins on opening weekend, from early morning to an evening gala Pullman with fireworks.

Other attractions included historic tours of East Grinstead High Street, a special charter railtour from London (page 127) and a locomotive naming, afternoon teas, guided shed tours, tours of Sheffield Park National Trust garden, vintage bus tour of closed railway stations, cheese and wine evening, rail ale evening, trip to Standen, thanksgiving service (page 126) and tours of St Giles Church Horsted Keynes and the Macmillan family grave.

Of course, after waiting so patiently to clear the tip after being dogged several times by the weather, what did it do on opening day? It snowed.

However, the railway had a fantastic opening festival and Easter period. If you haven't yet visited and taken a ride over the whole line, we look forward to seeing you soon!

Left: High above the rooftops: A Sheffield Park service leaves East Grinstead on 24 March. ANDREW STRONGITHARM

BR 9F No 92212 runs round its train to an appreciative audience at East Grinstead in preparation for the 11.15am departure on 23 March. DUDLEY HUBBARD

OPENING FESTIVAL

Tourist signage on the approaches to East Grinstead now include the Bluebell Railway. COLIN TYSON

Opening day… and the crowds arrive, despite the weather. JON BOWERS

First dog ticket to East Grinstead: 'Ripley' and owner and Bluebell Guide Nigel Simpkins are welcomed by the railway's chairman, Roy Watts as the first dog to arrive from Sheffield Park by timetabled service. Ripley had already walked over the viaduct (twice), travelled over it via diesel and completed the sponsored walk in February. TONI SIMPKINS

Nos 323 and B473 cross Imberhorne Viaduct with the 2.15pm service from East Grinstead on 1 April 2013. NICK GILLIAM

Service of Thanksgiving

Address given by Bishop Alan Chesters, formerly Bishop of Blackburn, as part of the Service of Thanksgiving at St Swithun's, East Grinstead, on Sunday 7 April 2013.

I am delighted to share in this celebration of the return of the Bluebell Railway and its steam locomotives to East Grinstead – the very town where the man who has gone down in history as the instigator of the demise of the branch line lived. When I was young and the Bible very much part of school life, enthusiasts spent idle moments seeking scriptural texts to support for their pastimes. Lovers of cricket found backing in Acts where they read 'Peter stood up and was bold'. Beer drinkers liked the text where 'Paul took courage'. Rail enthusiasts might turn to Isaiah's vision of God in which 'his train filled the temple'. From that we can surely justify coming to this holy place to thank God for the restoration of a railway line.

I think I owe my abiding passion for railways to the church. In the earliest sermon I can remember, the preacher in the Methodist chapel in the Pennines where I went to Sunday School claimed that when faced with life's challenges we should think of an engine, climbing a gradient, the clickety-click of the wheels seeming to say 'I am going to do it, I am going to do it' and then having reached the summit, gathering speed downhill, singing 'I have done it, I have done it'.

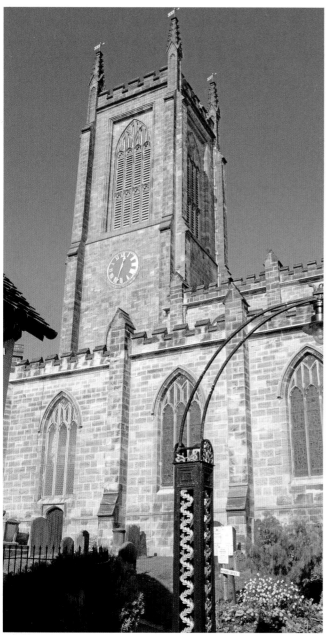

St Swithun's, East Grinstead. COLIN TYSON

Well, the Bluebell Railway has done it and we rejoice! When I became an Anglican, our parish priest was 'train mad'. Youth club trips were organised to the sheds at Doncaster and Crewe. Bishop Eric Treacy was our archdeacon, writing in my autograph book – 'good train spotting, stick to your Sunday School!' As if that was not enough indoctrination, 50 years ago when I was first ordained and the Bluebell Railway was in its infancy, our area Bishop of Kingston, William Gilpin, was a great supporter. Trips for curates were organised to Sheffield Park to ride on the restored line as part of their post-ordination training.

This is Eastertide as we celebrate Christ's resurrection from the dead with its promise of new life and hope for this world and the next and with that, the challenge to change things for the better. We may be forgiven for linking the restoration of something which seemed dead and finished, like the line from East Grinstead to Sheffield Park, and that unique resurrection of Jesus from the tomb which is at the heart of our Christian faith.

Have you ever wondered why so many Christians, not least clergy, are rail enthusiasts? This is more than nostalgia for the past. Whether we think of the first passenger line between Manchester and Liverpool, the building of rural railways across Sussex or the restoration of the Bluebell Railway, such projects begin with a vision – a vision of getting somewhere and opening up new possibilities and experience of life for many people, much as Isaiah had a vision of what he had to do for the people of Israel.

Christians often visualise life as a journey – a journey with ups and downs, joys and sorrows, challenges and solutions. John Bunyan called it *Pilgrim's Progress*. In Ely the Pickering tomb epitaph claims 'The Line to heaven by Christ was made, with heavenly truth the rails are laid, from earth to heaven the line extends, to eternal life where it ends'.

To have a vision of God's purpose is a terrific experience but usually to make a vision become reality will be costly. Cynics will ridicule, the apathetic will think it a pipe-dream. It will take courage and perseverance. It did for Isaiah when God called and he replied 'Here am I, send me'. Tonight we thank God for the vision of those who in the early 1970s came forward with the seemingly crazy idea that the line might be once more linked with the network at East Grinstead and so be accessible to more people. For many, contemplating the rubbish in Imberhorne Cutting and let us face it, the cost – millions of pounds, it must have seemed a vision too far, given the demands of the existing line. We thank God tonight not only for the 'vision of the few' but also for their persistence and patience over 25 years as they dealt not only with the terrain but with 30 different landowners. We give thanks for them, some of whom, like Bernard Holden, now rejoice with us in God's nearer presence.

The recent TV programmes on railways illustrated how many people must co-operate for trains to run. This completed Bluebell extension is the result of many, many, human hours by professionals and that army of volunteers – hundreds, thousands – getting stuck in, in practical ways, helping on the track or its stations, its fundraising and catering and much more. Again like the church, a railway, not least a heritage line, comes to life when people share their skills and their time working together to build something which will enhance the life experience of others. Tonight we thank God for all those people. It is an example of what can be achieved when people cooperate together as surely our Creator intended.

Some who do not share our enthusiasm may say would not the effort have been better spent in building a hospital rather than restoring a line which was not exactly profitable even in its heyday. They miss the point. It is a worthwhile activity to work together to bring enjoyment, happiness, simple pleasure to lives that are perhaps mundane, if not stressed. We trust in the Lord of life who enjoyed a party. The ultimate secret of the Christian Gospel is the promise of eternal joy through the Lord's offering on the Cross. The success of this project lies not just in reminding future generations of what a rural steam railway was like but in offering a time of relaxation and renewal to volunteer or fare paying passenger alike. For that to happen the need to volunteer, to work together, to share skills will continue when the thrill of achieving this arrival in East Grinstead is but a memory.

Tonight we thank God for what has been achieved and for those who have made it possible and pray that in some small measure this restoration, like the Lord's resurrection, will bring joy to many.

First through charter train and locomotive naming

by Nigel Longdon

History was made on 28 March 2013 when the first through charter train ran from London Victoria to Sheffield Park (via East Grinstead). This train was the first to travel the whole route since 1958. It was organised by UK Railtours, hauled by GBRf No 66739, and comprised 12 coaches and a pair of 73 Electro-Diesels at the rear to provide heating – these being Nos 73119 and 73207.

The '66/7' was an appropriate choice as these locomotives were used to haul our 'Waste by Rail' trains that removed some 80,000 tonnes of waste from Imberhorne Cutting.

On arrival at Sheffield Park, the train returned to Horsted Keynes where No 66739 was formally named *Bluebell Railway*. The BRPS crest is displayed on the right of the nameplate. *(The irony of a diesel running round with the words 'Let Steam Flourish' on the side has not been lost – Ed)*. A mounted copy of the nameplate was presented to the railway, where it is now on display in the museum. After the naming ceremony, the two 73s hauled a rake of Bluebell coaches on a series of service trains prior to the return of the whole charter train back to Victoria.

During the journey from Victoria, volunteers

Class 66 No 66739 arrives at Horsted Keynes on 28 March with Standard tank No 80151 as No 80154 to the left – a reminder of the last down train from East Grinstead in 1958. MIKE ESAU

from the on-train fundraising team were allowed to sell commemorative certificates to mark the occasion, raising a useful £800, and the on train raffle raised a further £1200 towards Northern Extension Project costs.

We thank John Farrow (UK Railtours) and John Smith (GBRf) for making the day possible. Hopefully there will be further opportunities to run through trains to Sheffield Park in the not too distant future.

66739 Bluebell Railway

Over 400 Class 66 locomotives were built in Canada for use in the UK and No 66739 was completed in February

PHIL BARNES

2004. New to Freightliner and numbered 66579, it later passed to Great British Railfreight (GBRf).

It weighs 126 tons and in April 2012 had a minor de-railment at Robertsbridge, East Sussex. No 66739 was repainted at Eastleigh at the beginning of 2013, prior to hauling the 'The Blue Belle' railtour on 28 March 2013.

Loco naming ceremony with (from left) Graham Flight plc chairman, Roy Watts BRPS chairman, John Smith managing director GBRf, Fr John Twisleton Bluebell Chaplain and Chris White, infrastructure director. ANDREW STRONGITHARM

The 3pm East Grinstead to Sheffield Park service on 'railtour day' approaches Imberhorne Cutting with Nos 73119 and 73207 and B473. PHIL BARNES

Newly-named No 66739 *Bluebell Railway* passes West Hoathly with the 4.50pm train from Horsted Keynes to London Victoria. MIKE ESAU

Next stop Ardingly?

Ardingly station in its full glory, looking east towards Horsted Keynes. COLIN TYSON COLLECTION

Formed of Hastings unit No 1001 and with No 73141 *Charlotte* leading, GBRf's 'The Wandering Willow' charity railtour of 30 October 2010 took in the Ardingly branch and is seen coming off the line to join the Brighton Main Line at Copyhold Junction. ANDREW STRONGITHARM

The small 117 yard viaduct immediately west of Horsted Keynes at Sheriff Mill was demolished in 1968. These are the surviving abutments at the Horsted Keynes end, seen in 2004. PHIL BARNES

While the Bluebell's first priority was the completion of its Northern Extension Project to East Grinstead, any westward extension from Horsted Keynes towards Ardingly and Haywards Heath would only follow a period of consolidation, for investment is now needed in a backlog of much-needed maintenance and repairs to the existing infrastructure, locos and rolling stock.

The line to Horsted Keynes from Haywards Heath via Ardingly opened on 3 September 1883 but the station's only busy times came with 'Rambler's specials' or the beginning and end of the College terms with the attendant items of trunks and luggage to deal with.

The branch was electrified in the 1930s, and in the final years up to closure in 1963 the line was served by 2-Hal and 2-Bil units which connected with Bluebell Railway steam trains across the platforms at Horsted Keynes. In the last years before closure the line was singled, with the non-operational track used for stock storage, most notably the new Kent Coast electric stock prior to its introduction, and subsequently the steam stock that it replaced, awaiting scrapping.

The trackbed from Horsted Keynes to the road bridge at Ardingly is in Bluebell ownership. This branch along with the 'main' line from buffer stop at Sheffield Park to buffer stop at East Grinstead, makes the Bluebell Railway the second largest private land owner in Sussex, after Gatwick Airport. The land purchase has been funded initially with a loan from a member and a wonderful response to an appeal to the membership.

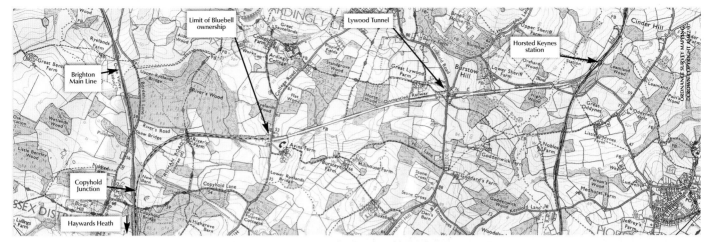

Looking west along the trackbed towards the 218-yard Lywood Tunnel in January 1998. **MIKE ESAU**

The land became available due to the break-up of the estate of which it was part.

For the moment, only the very basic maintenance is being carried out, with particular reference to encroachment, drainage and fencing.

The trackbed is in good condition, as is Lywood Tunnel. To re-open the line a missing short girder-bridge span needs replacing as will the small Sheriff Mill Viaduct, the condition of which was one of the reasons the line closed in 1963. A suitable span has been found and donated to the Bluebell Railway from a road project in North Wales.

The stub of the line from Haywards Heath still serves an aggregates depot at Ardingly, which occupies the former station platforms and goods yard. This has seen recent re-investment in plant, and there are several incoming aggregates trains a week. However, Bluebell should be able to extend through this site to re-connect with the main line, since a route along the edge of the site for its track has been safeguarded.

Recent re-signalling work at Horsted Keynes already allows a provision for the eventual re-laying of the line to Ardingly, thereby saving on 'doing the job twice'.

Much debate ensues regarding the option to re-electrify the branch, for use by preserved electric trains as well as Bluebell's own steam trains. This has not been ruled out but would be an expensive undertaking.

The Bluebell Railway's Long Term Plan

FUTURE EXTENSIONS

published in 2013 contains the following regarding the Ardingly branch:

a) Continue enabling works for the re-construction of the line from Horsted Keynes to Haywards Heath as finance and opportunities arise.

b) Maintain the drainage, fences, structures and trackbed to prevent further deterioration, and to perform an annual check of the boundary of our land, so as to prevent encroachment by third parties.

c) To encourage volunteer groups to maintain the trackside in a condition that will ease surveying, arrest deterioration, and help the eventual re-laying of the track.

d) Maintain a watching brief over proposed developments that might either compromise, or assist re-opening of the branch.

When Haywards Heath residents were questioned in June 2012 regarding the long term development of the town's Station Quarter, 71% agreed that safeguarding a facility for the arrival of the Bluebell Railway was 'important/very important'.

GOING SOUTH?

A southward extension towards Lewes has long been considered impractical due to the initial difficulty in bridging the raised, widened and re-aligned A275 main road immediately to the south of Sheffield Park station. While in the very long term an extension south from Sheffield Park might be feasible, that's really looking much too far into the future for anyone to consider, for at least the next half century.

At the A272 at Newick & Chailey, the cutting and station site have been reclaimed, and are incorporated into resident's back gardens. Even if it were possible to purchase that land, the cutting is itself filled with rubbish that would not be as easy to dispose of as that at Imberhorne as it includes industrial waste.

As part of its Long Term Plan, the railway is in support of the general principal that the remaining trackbed is a potentially valuable transport corridor which should be safeguarded if at all possible.

Is this the new Sheriff Mill Viaduct?

Matthew Taylor of the Highways Agency stands on one half of a rail bridge that currently rests in a motorway maintenance depot beside the M5. But until very recently the disused two span rail bridge crossed live traffic on the M50 in Worcestershire. The bridge is soon to be transported to South East England where it will be installed by the Bluebell Railway which has plans to reinstate steam trains on a branch line between Horsted Keynes and Ardingly (see Sketch P11).

"We placed an advertisement in a railway heritage magazine and got six responses, two of which were serious," said Mr Taylor. "The bridge would otherwise have gone to scrap but it seemed such a shame to waste it, so we decided to donate it to a good cause."

The bridge is in good condition with only cosmetic damage. Had it remained in place over the motorway the bridge would have represented additional maintenance cost for the Agency in future, he added. The bridge formed part of a little used branch line between Upton upon Severn and Ashchurch which closed in 1961, a year before the M50 opened.

**Hanson Aggregates
Ardingly Depot**

Above: A suitable single width bridge to span the gap at Sheriff Mill has been located as surplus to an M50 road scheme and donated to the Bluebell Railway – as highlighted in the *Transportation Professional Journal* for Jan/Feb 2013.

Left: An Amey Roadstone plant was established on the goods yard at Ardingly upon closure of the branch and, still rail served, survives under the ownership of Hanson plc. COLIN TYSON

Below left: GWR 'Dukedog' No 9017 arrives at Horsted Keynes from Oswestry via the Ardingly branch on 15 February 1962, a year before Horsted Keynes to Seaford electric trains ceased and the branch closed. BLUEBELL ARCHIVE

Below: The entrance to Lywood Tunnel, looking west. MIKE ESAU